IMPACT
CANADA
100

IMPACT CANADA 100

Taking the Spiritual and Moral Pulse of our Nation

By David Mainse

With Wendy E. Nelles

Forward by Don Moore
Executive Director, Vision 2000 Canada

CROSSROADS
Family of Ministries

P.O. Box 5100
Burlington, Ontario Canada L7R 4M2
(416) 335-7100 (Business)
(416) 335-0100 (Prayer)

1st Printing: July 1992 – 25,000
ISBN 0-921702-39-6 Soft Cover

Copyright © 1992 Crossroads Christian Communications Inc.

Published by Crossroads Christian Communications Inc.
P.O. Box 5100, Burlington, Ontario, Canada L7R 4M2

Cover Photo: Miller Comstock
Cover Design: Brad Moyer

Printed in Canada by
Harmony Printing Limited
123 Eastside Drive, Toronto, Ontario, Canada M8Z 5S5

"He shall have dominion also from sea to sea,
and from the river to the ends of the earth."
Psalm 72:8

My special thanks to Wendy Nelles who took my volumes of notes on 100 communities across Canada and helped me put it all together into a much more readable form than I could have done.

Also, on Friday, June 19th, I had the distinct honour of having our Prime Minister introduce me to President Boris Yeltsin. The Prime Minister told him about our T.V. efforts and I shared with President Yeltsin about the 15 Russian students coming to join us at the Crossroads Centre to study Christian television this September. It was a joy to see up close the chemistry at work between our leaders and the leader of Russia. It made me proud to be a citizen of a great country which cares about the needs of others.

"*Canadians, whatever you do, adhere to the Union. We are a great country and shall become one of the greatest if we preserve it. We shall sink into insignificance and adversity if we suffer it to be broken.*"

Sir John A. Macdonald (1815-1891)
Canadian Statesman and First Prime Minister
of the Dominion of Canada

O CANADA

O Canada! Terre de nos aïeux,
Ton front est ceint de fleurons glorieux!
Car ton bras sait porter l'épée,
Il sait porter la croix!
Ton histoire est une épopée
Des plus brillants exploits.
Et ta valeur, de foi trempée,
Protégera nos foyers et nos droits,
Protégera nos foyers et nos droits.

O CANADA

O Canada Our home and native land
True patriot love in all thy sons command
With glowing hearts we see thee rise
The true north strong and free
From far and wide O Canada we stand on
guard for thee
God keep our land glorious and free
O Canada, we stand on guard for thee
O Canada, we stand on guard for thee!

Words by R. S. Weir
Music by C. Lavallée

A COVENANT FOR CANADA

Sovereign Lord, ruler of all nations, we do humbly appeal to you to heal our land. You know our needs — for inspired leadership, for the restoration of Christian love at the heart of the family, for charity towards our neighbours, and for compassion towards those less fortunate than ourselves. You have helped us in the past; we pray that You will help us now, and in the future.

In the heart of each citizen, rekindle a fresh love of this land You have given us, and of all the unique peoples you have gathered here. In our constitution we recognize You as having dominion over us; it was You who fitly joined us together, and we pray that You will intervene to prevent us from being torn asunder.

Instill in each of us a renewed vision of what You intend us to become — as individuals and as Canadians — and show us what each of us must do to bring that vision to reality. In each of our lives there are places where we have fallen short of Your plan, or the living example of Your Son. We are sorry for those places, Father, and we ask Your forgiveness for them. Grant us the grace to amend our ways, that each of us might become a candle, to draw others to Your light. Then join our lights together, that we might become a beacon that will shine from sea to sea and draw all men to You, in this the planet's hour of greatest need.

To this end, before Your throne and in the sight of Your children, we do solemnly covenant to pray each day for Your divine grace and mercy to be poured out on this land. Help us, Lord, to become prayer warriors who will stand on guard for this Dominion. Help us to turn from those ways which have displeased you, and fill us with Your love for all our countrymen. Without Your assistance, we cannot survive, so hear us, O Lord, and heal our Land. In Jesus' name. Amen.

TABLE OF CONTENTS

FOREWORD

Canada's greatest need is for Christian leaders with vision and hope to reach our nation for Christ through commitment and cooperation. God wants to use men and women of prayer who, through creative and faith-stretching means, can bring about spiritual unity which will reflect the love of Christ which binds us together.

David Mainse is a classic example of one of Canada's few visionary leaders! Through his leadership of over 30 years, Crossroads Christian Communications Inc. has creatively reached into the homes and lives of literally thousands of Canadians with the healing message of the Gospel of Jesus Christ. Only in glory will we fully realize the extent to which God has used His servant and the wide range of Crossroads' ministries to touch the unreached.

As a well-respected leader in Canadian Christian broadcasting, David has contributed significantly to the spiritual fabric of our nation with integrity and excellence. He has sacrificially served countless other ministries through sharing the television programs, expertise and resources of the Crossroads Family of Ministries.

From the early formative days of Vision 2000 Canada, a movement committed to evangelism during this decade, David has made significant contributions, along with over 60 denominations and parachurch ministries, to see a new spirit of unity and commitment to evangelism emerge across Canada.

Probably the most energetic and high-profiled nationwide evangelistic initiative of this decade so far was accomplished through the IMPACT CANADA 100 tour taking the message of hope to one hundred communities across Canada. This book tells the memorable story of bringing the gospel to the grassroots of Canadian society.

David reflects on the foundations laid by our forefathers, adding his own unique perspectives on the past decade. Many

17

Canadians will remember that in 1981 David made his first nationwide tour called SALUTE TO CANADA. Now in retrospect, David is well-positioned to make significant observations on what is happening to our nation today.

Teaming up with the research being done by Vision 2000 Canada, David collected nearly 1000 surveys entitled "Listening to the Heartbeat of Canada's Church Leadership" which identified the hindrances churches are facing in evangelism. Using these important findings, David focuses, in this book, on the issues facing the church in Canada. He concludes with a tremendous sense of hope for what he sees will be significant spiritual changes in our nation during this decade.

Woven throughout this book, David makes statements which reflect the priority and importance of prayer. In my ongoing extensive travels across Canada, I must concur that I am witnessing a tremendous growing commitment to prayer for all levels of society. We are a divided country with fractured relationships on virtually every side. Canadians are desperately searching for hope and an answer to provide true meaning to life since their securities of the past have failed. Our responsibility, as God's people, is to demonstrate "unity to let the world know that you have sent me and have loved them even as you have loved me" (John 17:23 NIV). That unity and revival will only take place when we begin to fall to our knees admitting our own inadequacies and need of Him. The Old Testament records it best,

> "If my people, who are called by my name, will humble themselves and **pray** and **seek** my face and **turn** from their wicked ways, **then** will I **hear** from heaven and will **forgive** their sin and will **heal** their land" (2 Chronicles 7:14 NIV).

When that healing takes place, what ultimately made the IMPACT CANADA 100 tour so worthwhile will be our experience too! For during that tour David saw history made for over one thousand Canadians who began their new life in Christ under the preaching of the Word of God. To God be the glory for the great things He has done and will continue to do through the ministry of Crossroads!

As you read this book, may your hopes be increased and your vision expanded for what He can do by faith in **your** life to reach your neighbours for Christ. Together we, as God's people, can give every person in Canada the opportunity to see, hear and respond to the gospel by the year 2000.

Don Moore
Executive Director
Vision 2000 Canada

CHAPTER ONE

The Impetus Behind a Nationwide Campaign

I couldn't believe what I was witnessing on the nightly television news. Never in my life had I expected to see our Canadian Armed Forces troops in a military stand-off against fellow Canadian citizens, let alone against our native peoples. But there it was, night after night, graphic images of police officers, soldiers and Mohawk reserve residents, all dressed in battle fatigues, fingering loaded weapons, staring at each other across barbed-wire barricades.

I suppose that intellectually I had accepted the fact that Canada was in deep trouble when the Meech Lake efforts, which were designed to bring Quebec into the constitution, failed – but I didn't accept it emotionally until the land claims dispute at Oka and Kanesatake erupted into that armed confrontation.

I have always had the highest respect for the aboriginal peoples of Canada. I count a number of our first citizens as my very good friends, and we've worked together for a long time, particularly across the North. For many years, we've featured a "native peoples week" on *100 Huntley Street,* in which all our guest speakers and musicians are native Christians.

So the Oka crisis hit me with a real wallop. I found it hard to comprehend that I was witnessing the first armed military confrontation in Canada in over a hundred years. In June of 1990, it got me in the head; but in August, it got me in the heart. And it had all started over such a small thing – whether to expand a golf course. To me, it was a classic example of greed and the modern-day attitude of "what's in it for me." It was so diametrically opposite to the message of Christianity, where the most profound things are the simplest things – like loving your neighbour.

I couldn't stop pondering the situation, while I drove through the early morning darkness to the Huntley Street studios, between television tapings and planning meetings, and even while I was replacing rotted siding on the old barn at our farm. As I thought and prayed, I kept trying to come up with something I could do, as an individual, to be part of the solution – and not, because of apathy, to remain part of the problem.

Then an inspiration came to me. We'll go to the people. To the political and spiritual leaders of our nation, and to grass-roots Canadians. To adults and to children, our future generation of decision-makers. We'll visit 100 centres across our great land in the coming year. I knew it would be an ambitious and time-consuming agenda, but the crisis situation demanded the effort.

It was time to find a Christian perspective on the state of our nation. After all, the roots of the vast majority of our citizens are Christian. At this critical time of national uncertainty, we needed like never before to take a fresh look at those Biblical roots.

As a matter of fact, I couldn't help but think that our country was like the proverbial drunken sailor, staggering from crisis to crisis. Canada was sick; as a nation, we were in the emergency ward. But with a *Toronto Star* poll indicating that 80 percent of Canadians believed in a personal God who hears and answers prayer, there was a chance that people would be receptive to a divine prescription.

So, at the same time that government constitutional commissions were criss-crossing the country in search of a national identity, we set a goal to visit 100 towns and cities from the Pacific to the Atlantic in 1991. We travelled in a big old bus with a team of nine people, with musicians, with children's programs, and with gripping videos portraying both the problems and the potential of our great land.

Each night's two-hour program began with a panoramic videotape of glorious Canadian scenes on a big screen, featuring the rousing anthem, "He Shall Have Dominion". This theme song was composed by my son-in-law, Bruce Stacey, for the Vision 2000 Canada multi-denominational evangelistic thrust taking place throughout the 1990s, of which we were a part. Enthusiastic audience participation in singing grand old hymns and our national anthem preceded greetings from local dignitaries and pastors. A second video for the adults, "Is There Any Hope for our Future?", powerfully illustrated the critical issues facing all of us, ranging from economic uncertainty and unemployment to increasing violence, loss of traditional values and family breakdown.

The kids enjoyed their own program in a separate area, with music, animated videos, a message and a special appearance by Hiram Joseph as the voice of "Vibes", the minstrel from Crossroads' hit TV series *Kingdom Adventure*. In the "Vibes" body-suit most nights was John Whalen, one-time school principal and executive assistant to the late Honourable Joey Smallwood. John helped me organize the tour and was willing to do any job that was needed. When he would exit like the Pied Piper leading the children, I would often tell the crowd who it was in the costume. It never failed to get a laugh when I would say something like, "Unemployment is high, and when you need a job, you need a job!"

At every location, I made sure that we sang our national anthem, "O Canada". There's an interesting story behind this song. Most people, including the French-speaking radio hosts in Montreal on whose shows I appeared, didn't know this: "O Canada" was originally a French hymn and was being sung in French for 30 years before it was ever translated into English! As far as I'm concerned, the French version is a far more beautiful rendition, and it recognizes the Lord far more than the English first verse, even with "God keep our land" now added to the chorus.

Actually, before I started the tour, some "prophets of doom" were telling me that it would be impossible to hold any *Impact Canada 100* rallies in Quebec. I replied, "Quebec is part of Canada, and it's the province of my birth, so of course we're going to be there." To me, our rally in Montreal on June 25, 1991, was one of the highlights of the whole tour.

Those same doom-sayers had warned me, "Whatever you do, don't ask them to sing 'O Canada' if you do go to Quebec." That was all the incentive I needed to challenge the French- and English-speaking Montrealers in the audience to out-sing each other in volume. We were meeting in Le Tritorium, a large theatre auditorium. Our francophone song leader and our anglophone song leader each took a microphone and started, and the people just bellowed it out. The loudest "O Canada" we heard all across the country was that night in Montreal! Best of all, people came forward at the close of my message to give their lives to Christ. And I'll never forget that afterwards, a Muslim gentleman who had been present came up to us, and thanked us for what we were doing for Canada.

At every location, I determined that I would bring a message which would call each of us to individually search our own hearts. I knew that only by coming to that private place of genuine repentance could any of us determine to turn around our personal lives. And only by making a commitment to God, a commitment to really make a difference in our own lives, could we be made better people and, in turn, better Canadian citizens.

Now, don't get me wrong. By this, I didn't mean a superior attitude, or that we'd suddenly become better than everyone else around us. I meant that through the grace of God, we'd become more just and more loving human beings than we otherwise would have been in our own strength. After all, it was only love for God which could give any of us the power to get along with people and to follow the second greatest commandment, to love our neighbours as ourselves. It would take that kind of love for Canadians to make the compromises necessary to find the answers to the problems facing us.

But if we could just impact several thousands of people across the country to collectively make that kind of a commitment, to decide to become a better person, a better neighbour, a better voter, a more concerned and compassionate person for the needs of our society – well, just think of how that might affect each community and, in turn, our country at large!

I became excited by the potential. What would be the long-range repercussions if Canadian believers cultivated an enhanced sense of Christian responsibility toward their country? If we could have more empathy and understanding for people of other languages or races or cultures within our land? If we could make the effort to learn more about their hopes and dreams? If we could really love them as priceless individuals who are beloved of God?

Although a cross-country tour was a major undertaking, I wasn't doing this as a form of political activism. We deliberately had no political party and no political agenda in mind. As a matter of fact, I avoided anything which might appear like a partisan statement.

I just saw myself as a concerned Canadian who, using the platform given to me by the grace of God through the national television ministry, wanted to do what I could to help at a time of pessimism and disenchantment. And I remembered what Queen Elizabeth had said during one of her recent visits to our Dominion, "Canada is a country that has been blessed beyond many others. It's a country worth working for."

So off we went to city after city between January and September of 1991: Chilliwack, Campbell River, Medicine Hat, Camrose, Swift Current, North Battleford, Portage La Prairie, Brandon, Sarnia, Brockville, Montreal, Moncton, Dartmouth, Charlottetown, St. John's... to every location bringing the same message of repentance and restoration, for individuals and for a nation.

CHAPTER TWO

Looking Back at an Historical Perspective

I've always been sentimental about the vision of the Fathers of Confederation. Over the years, I'd made a personal acquaintance with our only living Father of Confederation, The Honourable Joseph R. Smallwood. Joey Smallwood had an incredibly contagious kind of fire and excitement about Canada. He had been a guest several times on *100 Huntley Street,* and we had shared many conversations about our country and our hopes and dreams for its future.

Actually, his younger sister, Mrs. Dorothy Collins, was the head captain for a number of years at our telephone counselling centre for *100 Huntley Street* in St. John's, Newfoundland. She led many people to Christ during that time. I was hesitant to recount my memories of Joey Smallwood, but Dorothy has graciously agreed to share this very special story with you.

Joey first appeared on the Dominion Day program of *100 Huntley Street* in 1978, during which he said wonderful things like "God bless Canada!" and "God keep Quebec in Canada!" That night, when my wife Norma-Jean was driving him back to his hotel, she said to him, "Joey, please give your life to Jesus. Canada needs you as our only living Father of Confederation to be strong for God. Your personal testimony of faith could mean so much to Canadians." Tears came down his cheeks, but he shook his head and said, "No, I'm afraid I couldn't live it."

This same reaction happened several times over the years. I know that Mr. Smallwood was a great admirer of the eighteenth-century English evangelist and theologian John Wesley, who founded Methodism. I think that because Wesley had set

26

such high standards for righteousness, Joey was perhaps afraid that no one could live up to them, and he didn't want to be a hypocrite.

I'll let Dorothy take over the story from here:

David happened to be in Newfoundland at the time when Joey was first taken with a stroke five years ago. He had been rushed to the hospital in St. John's the night before, and he wasn't supposed to have any visitors except family. However, David asked me if I could get permission to visit Joey. I made arrangements with the nurse for David to come in.

When David came into the hospital room, Joey was lying in bed, listening to a cassette tape. The stroke had taken his speech, but he immediately recognized David, and his mind was still very alert. David said to him, "Mr. Smallwood, do you remember when Norma Jean begged you to give your life to Jesus and you said you felt you couldn't live it? Well, you've always been very blunt with people, so I'm going to be very blunt with you right now." Joey nodded his head.

David said gently, "There's not much sinning you can do from that position, Mr. Smallwood." He nodded his head yes again, and tears started to flow down over his face, wetting the pillow beneath his head. David asked him if he would like to give his heart to the Lord, and told him to squeeze his hand if he understood. Joey did.

I'm going to pray a simple little sinner's prayer," David told him, "and you know as well as I do how to ask for salvation. You can pray your own prayer, or follow along after me." So David just said, "Lord, be merciful to me a sinner. Lord, forgive me of my sin. Come and live in my life. Whatever is left of my life, Lord, I give it to you." When David asked, "Mr.

Smallwood, did you pray that prayer with me with all your heart?", he nodded his head up and down, the tears still coming.

Months later, when I was visiting Joey in his home one day, I asked if he remembered the incident, and he indicated yes, that was when he gave his heart to the Lord. He never was able to speak after the stroke until the time of his death, but the family could understand his gestures. When I asked him if he was ready to meet the Lord, he nodded his head yes.

Joey passed away on December 22, 1991, just two days before his ninety-first birthday on Christmas Eve. What a thrill it was to be at his funeral at the Roman Catholic Basilica of St. John's and have that precious memory. It was a powerful service. Clergy of all denominations took part; the Prime Minister was there, as was Jean Chretien and the Newfoundland Premier Clyde Wells; and I just felt that even at the funeral, as these men shook hands, God was doing something. You know, Joey passionately loved Canada. He was the one who brought Newfoundland kicking and screaming into Confederation.

I share that passionate love for our country, and I have a deep concern for our political leaders. That was a major impetus for deciding to undertake the *Impact Canada 100* national tour, to bring a message of hope and of restoration. I wanted to make sure that my motives would not appear partisan in any way, so I determined that I would first meet with the leaders of all three major political parties which have standing in the House of Commons: the Prime Minister, Mr. Brian Mulroney; the Leader of the Opposition, Mr. Jean Chretien of the Liberal party; and the Leader of the New Democratic Party, Ms. Audrey McLaughlin. We displayed photographs of these meetings in the foyer of the auditoriums wherever we held our *Impact Canada 100* crusades, so that people coming in would realize I was speaking from a neutral platform, and was not there to campaign in support of any one party or group. During the tour, I also tried to meet as many of our provincial leaders as possible, including the premiers and the leaders of the opposition.

I wanted to be truly above party politics. Our call was universal, to all Canadians to endeavour to become better citizens, and to get involved in our country's future by supporting the political leaders of their choice. It seemed to me that our political leaders were not suffering from any deliberate intent to do evil, but from a lack of support.

As well-known Canadian Christian author, researcher and social analyst, Don Posterski, put it in the video we showed at *Impact Canada 100* pastors' luncheons, "If I were a political leader in Canada, I think I would go to bed every night and have nightmares. In Canada right now it's very difficult to lead, because leaders are not being supported, they're being attacked. You would think that most Canadians believe that politicians get out of bed in the morning and say, 'I think I'm going to try to make life difficult for people today,' or 'I'm going to get up and see what damage I can do today.'"

As the audience smiled, realizing the absurdity of that scenario, Don urged them, "I'm not here to affirm everything that political leaders are doing, but I am saying, 'Fellow Canadians, it's time for us to figure out who we're going to support, rather than just who we're going to attack.'"

My approach throughout the tour was encouraging Canadians to "find somebody in politics who you can believe in and get involved; go to work for them, whatever the party." As a result, some of the media people on local open-line radio programs, on television talk shows and in newspaper interviews may have found me a little boring, because I refused to take sides against one political leader or another.

But through this same "un-newsworthy" neutrality, I was able to meet and talk with both the Prime Minister and the Premier of Newfoundland, Mr. Clyde Wells, the two leaders who seemed to be on the opposite poles of the Meech Lake constitutional effort. During our conversation, I asked Mr.

Wells, "Tell me, if you will, behind those closed doors at the Meech Lake deliberations with yourself, the Prime Minister and the other provincial leaders – did anyone suggest prayer, even a brief time of silent prayer?" And he shook his head and said four times, very sadly, "No. No. No. No."

So I was particularly thankful that I was able to share an historical anecdote with Mr. Wells, with the Prime Minister and with several provincial leaders. To me, this story about prayer and the American folk hero Ben Franklin illustrates a pivotal turning point in U.S. history which had great spiritual significance.

I reminded these Canadian leaders that our neighbour to the south had faced just such a crisis two centuries before, in the American version of Meech Lake.

By the grace of God, the Thirteen Colonies had wrested their independence from the most powerful nation on earth. But in 1787, as delegates from the new States met in Philadelphia to frame a constitution under which they would consent to be governed, they seemed to have forgotten God. Quarreling and suspicious, they had squandered nearly all the goodwill they had brought with them. Everyone agreed that there had to be a Congress of elected representatives, but none could agree on its composition. Smaller States feared domination by larger ones; rural sectors were leery of commercial interests in the rapidly growing population centers imposing their wills. Some States had gone so far as to erect tariff barriers against their neighbors, as if they were separate nations. A few had even sent ambassadors abroad.

The situation in Independence Hall was grim. Once the States had trusted one another; their very survival had depended on it. But after eight weeks of wrangling, what little trust remained was rapidly running out, like the last grains of sand in an hour-

glass. Delegates from New York had already quit in disgust and gone home; others were on the verge of doing the same. The convention seemed doomed; in a few more days they would leave as they had come – a loose confederation bound together by a rope of sand.

In a few more years, regions presently pursuing exclusive trading arrangements with foreign powers might find themselves absorbed by same. The Liberty Tree, a favorite symbol of the young republic, was to have put down its tap-root at this constitutional convention. Without it, the tree would be uprooted by the first gale-force wind to come its way.

Ben Franklin was in despair. In this same room eleven years before, he and fifty-five others had signed a new nation into being. The United States of America – so disunited were they now, the name seemed a tragic irony. Franklin caught the eye of chairman George Washington, who bade the next speaker defer to him.

With difficulty the eighty-one-year-old scientist-philosopher got to his feet, and leaning on his silver-tipped walking stick, he addressed the General. "How has it happened, sir, that we have not hitherto once thought of humbly applying to the Father of Lights to illuminate our understanding?"

The hall grew still; Franklin was widely known for his enlightened agnosticism which had become the fashion. "In the beginning of the contest with Britain, when we were sensible of danger, we had daily prayers in this room for Divine protection. Our prayers, sir, were heard. And they were graciously answered. All of us who were engaged in the struggle must have observed frequent instances of a superintending Providence intervening in our favor..." he looked around the room at others of the original signers, *"and have we not forgotten this powerful Friend? Or,"* he smiled sadly, *"do we imagine we no longer need His assistance?"*

In the stunned silence, Franklin peered at Washington over the spectacles he had invented. *"I have lived, sir, a long time. And the longer I live, the more convincing proofs I see of this truth: that God governs in the affairs of men. And if a sparrow cannot fall to the ground without His notice, is it probable that an empire can rise without His aid?"*

A breeze stirred the green velvet draperies. Old Ben's voice grew resolute. *"We have been assured, sir,"* he declared, well aware of Washington's own deep faith, *"in the sacred writings that except the Lord build the house, they labor in vain that build it. I firmly believe this. I also believe that without His concurring aid, we shall succeed in this political building no better than the builders of Babel; we shall be divided by our little, partial, local interests, our projects will be confounded, and we ourselves shall become a reproach and a byword down to future ages."* He paused. *"And what is worse, mankind may hereafter, from this unfortunate instance, despair of establishing government by human wisdom and leave it to chance, war, or conquest."*

The General solemnly nodded, and the aged statesman concluded: *"I therefore beg leave to move that henceforth, prayers imploring the assistance of Heaven and its blessings on our deliberations, be held in this assembly every morning, before we proceed to business."*

No one seconded the motion; no one breathed a whisper. In the protracted silence that followed, all reflected on what he had said. It was true: when their lives had literally hung in the balance (Brit-

ain's traditional response to rebellion was the gallows) prayer had come easily. And with it, trust. And with trust, unity.

While they did not act immediately in a formal way upon Franklin's appeal, it nonetheless brought a shift in the convention's mood. As if someone had turned the hourglass, trust began to run back into their deliberations. And with it, a miraculous inspiration: why not a bicameral legislature? Two houses of Congress – the lower one comprised of Representatives according to population; the upper one, of two Senators from each State. It was a heaven-sent solution – for which more than a few privately thanked the Friend whose aid Franklin had so movingly invoked.

It seemed to me that in 1991, at the opening of the last decade of the second millennium after the birth of Christ, Canada was facing a similar situation. We had lost our trust of one another, and with it, our sense of national unity. Our Dominion was threatening to divide – ethnically, economically, and possibly even politically.

During this period of disintegration, we were lapsing into regionalism and tribalism, where we were only concerned about protecting ourselves and our own territory. We could witness it happening in Europe, where "balkanization" was seeing former confederations break apart into little groups, often at the cost of hatred, violence, bloodshed and irreparable loss.

What would the future hold here? Canadians were becoming more and more preoccupied with what was good for them personally and regionally, without regard for the whole. Radical changes in attitude were needed in order to reach consensus, but no one was willing to give an inch.

I was convinced that there was a remedy, the same that Ben Franklin so eloquently proposed. It may seem outmoded and unfashionable, or it may not occur to our leaders in their human wisdom to seek a supernatural solution. But God had promised in 2 Chronicles 7:14, "If my people who are called by my name will humble themselves and **pray** and seek my face, and turn from their wicked ways, then I will hear from heaven, and will forgive their sin and heal their land."

If you look at that historical vignette from a standpoint of spiritual perception, you will grasp how that call to prayer was instrumental in the American constitutional crisis. Of course, any historian who does not have a spiritual depth of understanding will always miss the important turning points in history. You know, so many people may physically grow up to be adults, but spiritually they are still at the stage of 12-year olds when they were confirmed, or when they dropped out of Sunday School because they were sure they'd learned it all. This means that in terms of spiritual maturity, many people today – including some of society's leaders – are adolescents, trying to be adults physically, mentally and emotionally, but with a vital part of their lives undeveloped or altogether missing.

I am positive that the crucial points in history are **spiritual,** not just sociological developments or political events or fate or luck. They are deliberate decisions which emanate from someone's spirit – whether it be a decision of darkness like Hitler, or a decision of light like the founders of Canada who made that verse from Psalm 72:8 our motto, "He shall have dominion also from sea to sea, and from the river to the ends of the earth."

CHAPTER THREE

Through the Eyes of Our Political Leaders

Before we embarked on *Impact Canada 100,* I wanted to speak privately with the three federal leaders – Mr. Mulroney, Mr. Chretien and Ms. McLaughlin – to inform them that we'd be meeting with several thousand members of the clergy in large and small centres, and to ask the leaders what they'd say, given the chance, to these front-line workers in our society.

So often, those in political leadership don't get the opportunity to express themselves on the deeper issues of faith. But each of the federal leaders I met with was positive that the church could be an essential part of the solution to the problems facing our nation. While each of them approached his or her faith in God a little bit differently, I sensed that they all were keenly aware of the need for a moral awakening in our land. And with the last of these conversations with federal leaders taking place the evening before allied forces unleashed the opening air attacks of the Gulf War, the need for prayer was never more gripping.

* * *

My appointment with the Prime Minister was set for 5:30 p.m., but it was already 6:05 p.m. or so when he finally came out of the House of Commons. It was one week before the Gulf War started, and he was immediately surrounded by a scrum of reporters, all firing questions at him about Canada's role in the rapidly-building Middle-East crisis. He bounded up the stairs – the same ones which we always see on the nightly newscasts – and I was waiting around the balcony on the other side. Now, with the lateness of the hour and all the issues on his mind, he could have easily slipped straight into his office and ignored me. Instead, he deliberately looked for me and invited me to come in.

I couldn't believe it: he gave me an hour and a quarter, and finally I was the one who broke it up. I said, "I understand, Prime Minister, that your wife is waiting with dinner for you, so please don't allow us to take your family time. I believe in the family, and you need them at this difficult time." Mr. Mulroney replied, "Oh, I've got to tell you just one more story before you go."

Apparently, a few days before, his youngest son Nicolas, who would have been five at the time, announced at the family dinner table that they were going to say grace in their family from now on. This was quite an admission, because obviously he and Mila had not been saying a blessing before meals up till then.

When the Prime Minister asked Nicolas where he had gotten that idea, he wouldn't say; he just repeated adamantly, "We are going to say grace in our family." So Mr. Mulroney gulped and said, "O.K., let's bow our heads and Nicolas, you say grace." Apparently the young boy had heard grace at the home of one of his friends, because when he tried to repeat one of the old memorized blessings, he ended up getting some of the words backwards! But anyway, the Prime Minister told me that, "We've been saying grace in our family ever since." I told that story almost every night at *Impact Canada 100* rallies, and people would always laugh and clap.

At one point during our interview, I thanked the Prime Minister, stating that I believed his wonderful family life – with the obvious closeness between himself, Mila and their four children Caroline, Benedict, Mark and Nicolas – was setting a good example to Canadians about the importance of keeping the family together and strong. You know, I was fascinated to note that during our time together, Mr. Mulroney's hand kept resting on the little wooden side table beside his chair, which held framed photographs of his wife Mila and of his children.

Three or four times throughout the hour, his hand would drift over to the photographs and he would gently caress the edge of the frame around Mila's picture. We were discussing the cynicism in the country, and he would be concentrating on a totally unrelated line of thought – yet it seemed like his body language was unconsciously saying, "Here's someone who believes in me. Here's someone who doesn't question my motives, who knows me better than anyone else. Here's someone who is loyal and who is faithful."

I couldn't help but think of the old Biblical term "helpmeet" which is used to refer to a man's wife, and I was sure that our Prime Minister was drawing strength from his relationship with his spouse. Obviously, they were deeply in love, and that was the strength which enabled him to function as Prime Minister with the lowest poll ratings at that particular point since they started to take opinion surveys. And yet, he still held his head up and walked with dignity.

Mr. Mulroney lamented the cynicism which Canadians seem to have about all institutions, not just government. His message was a challenge: "You've got to believe in somebody. Whether it's me or one of the other leaders, support somebody." He urged me to ask Christians to attend the constitutional hearings taking place across Canada and to make their views known. He also encouraged all Canadians to exercise understanding and generosity toward one another.

The Prime Minister spoke with great feeling about his love for Canada, his desire to "do what is right for our nation," and his hopes for national unity. He told me, "The one thing that Audrey McLaughlin, Jean Chretien and myself all have in common – and I truly believe this with all my heart – is that all of us passionately love Canada."

We didn't tape these interviews with political leaders, or take notes. I decided that deliberately, because I wanted it to be communication from the heart, not the head. Lots of people have wanted appointments to speak from the head, but not many have gone in from the heart, just to say, "Prime Minister, may I pray with you personally? May I pray for your health and strength? May I pray for your family, and for your responsibilities of Prime Minister?"

The next day, the Deputy Chief of Staff telephoned with the message that Mr. Mulroney had very much appreciated the meeting, especially its timing at that critical juncture, and that he had found it to be a source of strength and encouragement. The official also commented that for the Prime Minister to have spent that much time with a visitor was indeed an unusual event.

* * *

My appointment with Ms. Audrey McLaughlin had taken place at four p.m., several hours before I saw the Prime Minister. She was very gracious with her time and gave me as long as she possibly could. We talked about the fact that Bay Street stockbrokers and financiers couldn't be allowed to determine the bottom line for government action; instead, the national agenda had to be based on human need. I shared with her Scripture passages dealing with that concept. She also called Christians to social action, saying, "Tell them to be doers of the Word and not hearers only. Speak up when you see social injustice." But after about 20 minutes, a knock came at the door from one of her assistants, insisting that she was needed for an urgent briefing about the Gulf crisis before she had to face the Parliament Hill reporters.

We have to understand that these were crisis days in Parliament. It meant a great deal for these people to sacrifice their time. And it probably made them more open to prayer than ever before. After all, no one had any idea what Saddam Hussein could unleash with the Iraqi weapons arsenal. In January 1991, the world still wasn't sure how the Soviet Union would react. It potentially could have been the beginning of World War III.

I'll never forget when, one week later, U.S. President George Bush sent in the troops to invade Kuwait. We were all glued to our television sets across Canada and witnessed, one after another, the Prime Minister, the Leader of the Opposition and the Leader of the New Democratic Party, each stand up in the House of Commons and ask Canadians to pray.

It's interesting that in other crises, prayer hadn't always been requested. If I had not been with these people within the previous seven days, I would probably have been skeptical and thought to myself, "Well, they're just asking for prayer because it seems like the politically correct thing to do right now." But I had sensed their urgency when I asked them, "May I pray with you," and they had each replied, "Please, by all means." It was an enthusiastic and genuine invitation for prayer, and I really believe that God did hear and answer us.

* * *

Jean Chretien ushered me into his office on the Wednesday evening before war was declared. It was just a few days before I would embark on the *Impact Canada 100* tour in Langley, BC. It was also the end of his first day in which he had taken his seat in the House of Commons as official Leader of the Opposition. I thanked him for his previous efforts to keep Canada out of the war, on behalf of all Canadians who served in the Armed Forces. Although Mr. Chretien had believed that Canada should stay out of the conflict if we wanted to retain our "honest broker" position as mediator in world affairs, he immediately backed the Prime Minister as soon as the government had made its decision to commit our troops. I am so thankful that no Canadians were killed in action.

I then proceeded to ask Mr. Chretien what he perceived as the greatest need of Canadians. He replied, "Compassion and caring about others. People are too selfish. We've got to be more generous and start to give more to others." He was child number 19 in a large northern Quebec family; growing up during the depression years, he would know all about sharing. I shared with Mr. Chretien something which I knew about our first liberal Prime Minister of Canada, Alexander Mackenzie, whom passersby would see praying on his knees three times a day through the open door of his office on Parliament Hill. Mackenzie had been converted in Scotland before emigrating to Canada. When he came to Canada, he did very well as a businessman, and also became quite a social activist.

It is said that Mackenzie would walk the streets of Toronto in the 1850s during a bad economic depression, and find a man without work who had a family to support. He'd bring him home, put him up for the night, give him a bath and a meal and a new set of clothes, take him out early in the morning, and find him a job through friends in business. Clearly he was deeply involved in meeting social needs. Sir John A. MacDonald may have been the famous visionary, but Mackenzie was the practical man who stepped in to make things work for this country when he replaced Canada's first Prime Minister.

I told Jean Chretien that Mackenzie would no doubt today be considered a Christian fundamentalist, and modern society is fond of laying all kinds of troubles on the doorsteps of fundamentalists. But the British Prime Minister whom Mackenzie admired very much was Gladstone, who authored the classic book *The Impregnable Rock of Holy Scripture*. Gladstone was to a great extent responsible for the first colony in history to ever gain its independence without a shot being fired: Canada. Because Gladstone had certain principles in his life as a devout Christian, because he believed that God loved people, he was able to develop an outlook – not of an empire-builder or a power-monger – but of a conciliator.

Actually, politicians – as well as the public and the press –sometimes forget that so-called fundamentalist Christians started many of the major social movements which have impacted our twentieth century. And of course, we have to remember that it was the same Protestant, Alexander Mackenzie, who launched the career of Wilfrid Laurier, Canada's first French-Canadian, Roman Catholic Prime Minister. Obviously, being a "fundamentalist" committed Christian believer did not make him a bigot. Actually, the word "fundamentalist" has been ruined by twisted use. Perhaps it would be better to say that Mackenzie was a "hot" Christian, because Scripture tells us there are only three kinds: "hot, cold and lukewarm."

Coincidentally, Jean Chretien had to be hospitalized for surgery shortly after our visit; I have a feeling that he may have meditated on some of the things we talked about.

* * *

When I met with Canada's political leaders, I wasn't going there as a lobbyist. I went in there as an individual Canadian with my heart on my sleeve. I just wanted to tell them personally, "I love Canada, and I'm praying for you, and I represent a lot of other people who are praying for you. Can we pray together right now?" I was told afterward by some of their assistants that no one had ever asked to pray personally with these politicians like that before.

It may be hard to believe, but **not one** of the federal or provincial leaders refused to join me in prayer. They all revealed that they were feeling an immense burden of responsibility, and they welcomed prayer for divine wisdom. Some even talked about their childhood or disclosed personal struggles with their faith, or lack of faith.

I was actually flabbergasted during my meeting with Premier Don Getty of Alberta. When I asked him if we could pray together, he asked if I would like to kneel. I said, "Oh, yes," and we turned around to face the couch. There were two doors open into his office through which staff members could observe us, and out of the corner of my eye I certainly noticed some startled looks!

News of the meeting appeared in newspapers across Canada, as Canada Press picked up on the story, headlining it, "The power of prayer can help knit Canada together." The Premier was quoted as saying that he has often turned to prayer when faced with hardship. "Both in my public life and my personal life, my family and I have often faced some pretty strong challenges when we have turned to prayer and to God to receive the strength and inspiration which He can give you."

Mr. Getty went on to say, "I think when our country is under stresses and strain and the potential for disunity, it would do us all well if we asked that the Lord, who rules this entire dominion from sea to sea, would be there with us, helping us."

Of course, several papers such as the Edmonton Sun labelled the premier "Bible Don Getty" and questioned his motives, but a few weeks later, my friend Harry Rusk, a native Canadian who was recently inducted into the Country Music Hall of Fame, shared a note which he had received from Mr. Getty. In it, the Premier had written: "It certainly was my pleasure to take part in the *Impact Canada 100* tour hosted by David Mainse. It was an extremely uplifting experience and made me feel good inside."

Even though the other politicians didn't ask to kneel for prayer, I sensed that they were all mentally kneeling before God, admitting, "It's beyond us. We don't have the answers. We need God." Basically, I just led everyone in an extemporaneous, "heart-on-my-sleeve" type of prayer. I wasn't there to impress anybody except God. I prayed that each leader would experience God's provision and the promises of God. The Lord has told us that if anyone lacks wisdom, if we ask it of Him he will give it liberally, and not chastise us for the mistakes of the past.

* * *

Awareness of the promises of God was a recurring theme throughout *Impact Canada 100*. It was significant that the Prime Minister had concurred with me that Canada was founded on Christian principles. Many of us have read the inscription carved in stone at the base of the Peace Tower on Parliament Hill, which quotes Psalm 72:8, "He shall have dominion from sea to sea." Mr. Mulroney mentioned that he often looks at another verse on the wall in the Cabinet Room, over the portrait of Sir John A. MacDonald, "Without a vision, the people perish," from Proverbs 29:18.

I consider the seventy-second Psalm to be Canada's Psalm. I read it in its entirety every night during our *Impact Canada 100* meetings. Some nights I would preach on it. Its content reminded me of the lawyer-turned-evangelist Charles Finney, whose favourite text was found in Isaiah 28:17 where it says that, "Righteousness shall be thy plumb line and justice thy measuring line." In the Bible, righteousness and justice are inseparably intertwined. The great prophets of the past who addressed the political leaders and the people of their times never separated the two. Finney preached over and over again on that text, and whole communities in the Northern United States would turn to Christ and repent of their sin because of that theme. In some places, drunkenness became almost non-existent, courts had no cases to try and prisons were closed. Several states turned against slavery, eradicated child labour and began universal education.

Of course, today the word "justice" keeps recurring in our constitutional talks, as we seek justice for our native peoples, justice for our minority groups, justice for our French-speaking and our English-speaking peoples. But I believe that you can't have justice without righteousness. If that plumb-line – that vertical relationship with the Almighty God which causes us to have right horizontal relationships with mankind – is not in place in our lives, then true justice isn't possible. The first verse of Psalm 72 tells us, "Give the king **your** judgements, O God, and **your** righteousness the King's Son." That verse is also inscribed in Canada's Houses of Parliament.

I believe with all my heart that God takes these Scriptural inscriptions seriously. Our country was committed to God from the time of its founding. And we've seen further evidences of this since 1867: both our Bill of Rights in 1960 and our Charter of Rights and Freedoms in 1982 stated that Canada is a country founded on principles which recognize the supremacy of God. When Parliament revised the English wording of "O Canada" to make it a little closer to the French original a few years ago, and inserted the prayer, "God keep our land", I remember thinking to myself that all was not lost. Ironically, the only M.P. who voted against it in the House of Commons, I've been told, was a former clergyman!

CHAPTER FOUR

From the Vantage Point of a Decade

In reflecting on our *Impact Canada 100* tour, I find myself looking back even further to our *Salute to Canada* project ten years earlier. In 1981, we had launched a trans-continental salute to this nation, where in 31 days we travelled from sea to sea, broadcasting live from 25 different cities, including Ottawa and all the provincial capitals. At a time when regional interests were simmering to the surface, I had felt that the symbolism of broadcasting on-site across the nation was a God-given vision.

Salute to Canada was hailed by the press as "one of the greatest and most ambitious adventures in the history of Canadian television broadcasting." It really was a world's first, technologically speaking, and represented the largest undertaking to date by a transportable earth station. The people from Telesat Canada urged us to list the feat in the Guinness Book of World Records, but we haven't done it yet.

Our outdoor surroundings were featured on *100 Huntley Street* daily, as our broadcasts were beamed from the lawns of Victoria's Legislative Building, from a Rocky Mountain sunrise in Jasper, from the streets of Regina and Winnipeg, from Parliament Hill in Ottawa, from a terrace overlooking old Quebec City, from the docks of Halifax, from the harbour at St. John's and, on July first, from Province House in Charlottetown, where confederation had become a reality. There, we sang "O Canada," and as we came to the line "God keep our land," we released 115 red helium balloons – one for each year in which He had done so in His faithfulness.

The Saint John, New Brunswick *Evening Times Globe* said, "Whatever you want to call it, the idea of a 25 city, live broadcast of a daily Christian TV program – at a time when the country seems at political odds with itself, and at a time when religious apathy has never been so crushing – is truly an inspired idea."

Over a decade later, people still speak of that great trans-Canada adventure. Many, unable to make such a trip themselves, say that nothing else has so drawn the country together for them and made them feel so proud to be a Canadian. But the most important result was the spiritual dimension; we had been on a prayer pilgrimage, in the truest sense of the word. It had been our leading to bring the nation's prayer needs to the people, literally going out into the highways and byways, and raising the level of God-consciousness wherever we could.

In 1981, Canada was already a nation in torment, struggling to define its identity and become something which its far-flung, diverse citizens could whole-heartedly embrace. There was a lot of talk, back then, of the population being a vertical mosaic. But the tiles were coming loose, and the rough edges, instead of smoothing one another, were abrading. Even then, the debate about the need for a new constitution was a divisive issue. In many regions, people were so angry at Ottawa that they felt isolated and misunderstood, like strangers in a strange land.

As I reread what I wrote eleven years earlier in *God Keep Our Land,* I am struck by how little progress has been made by human attempts at mediation and compromise. Sad to say, the words remain just as applicable in the year in which we are marking the 125th anniversary of our nation's founding:

> My emphasis on the urgency of the regional interests caused me to reflect again on the desperate political climate in which Canada now found itself. In Quebec, the movement to separate that province from the rest of Canada had suddenly been revitalized. And yet as grave as that situation was, every bit as critical was the utter frustration felt by Albertans and other

western Canadians. They, and to a lesser extent, the Maritimers at the opposite end of the country, felt like forgotten peoples, without any significant influence in Ottawa, the seat of government. Indeed, it did not seem an exaggeration to say that never in the 114-year history of this nation, had we been so divided and splintered and set against one another. And as Jesus said so clearly, a house divided against itself could not stand. Unless something changed drastically – and soon – there was a real question as to whether Canada, as we knew it, would survive.

Patriotism, in the best sense of that word, simply did not have the uniting and rallying power that I had noticed in the States. And it was not hard to understand why: they had been bonded and annealed together in the furnace of the Revolutionary War and the Civil War. The concept of a permanent, "indissoluble" union was so ingrained that if any state were to suggest seceding, it would be taken as a joke. The "melting pot" had been around too long for that, and had done its work. Americans were Americans, not Italians or Poles or English or French or Germans, living in America.

But secession was no joke in my own Canada. The melting-pot principle had not been at work here. Instead of discarding their past and eagerly taking up English as their common tongue, newcomers retained their ethnic identities, until in many areas they were no longer minorities at all. There was, of course, a tremendous advantage to this: Canada was thus imbued with a depth and variety of cultural heritage far beyond her 115 years. Indeed, the richness of our societal mosaic was perhaps our greatest national treasure. Yet it also made for a much more fractionable society – one that simply could not be drawn together by conventional patriotic appeal.

In fact, it suddenly struck me, the **only** uniting force available in Canada was Jesus Christ. "God help us," some politician had recently exclaimed, "only He can, now!" And there was more truth in that than he may have seen: **the only solution left to a country that was literally tearing itself apart, was a spiritual one.**

Nor was that mere rhetoric: there **was** a viable solution. Regardless of how many languages one heard in the heart of a major Canadian city, or how tightly knit its ethnic groupings, there was one common meeting-ground – at the foot of the Cross of Jesus Christ. Kneeling there, one heard only one language, no matter how many tongues it might be spoken in. There was no class differentiation, no levels of rich or poor, educated or illiterate, no stratas of society. There were only sinners, with no choice between them.

Canada might never be united nationalistically, as the U.S. was, but she could be united spiritually... and perhaps that union would prove the strongest of all.

* * *

Looking back, I can say that we'd had a tremendous response in 1981 to *Salute to Canada*. It was reckoned that two-thirds of Canada tuned in to the Salute at one time or another. We had large and enthusiastic audiences every day, in all 25 communities we visited; there would be large banners out, saying "Welcome to Edmonton," or wherever, and one farmer even cut a greeting into a patch of hay! It was delightful.

Now, I don't mean to be unkind here, but in retrospect I'd say that a lot of the people who came out in 1981 were interested in being blessed themselves. They came to enjoy the music and the speakers, to show support for Crossroads, to celebrate our national heritage, and to be part of television history in the making. In contrast, ten years later I noticed a distinct difference in the people attending: it seemed that they were really concerned for Canada, and they wanted to pray for our nation. They weren't showing up just because some guy they'd seen on TV was coming to town.

The *Salute to Canada* tour had taken place shortly after the 1980 Quebec referendum, and there'd been a kind of starry-eyed optimism about our nation's future. But within a few months, the next era of Canadian history was starting to take shape, symbolized in 1982 by the repatriation of Canada's new constitution.

By 1991, no one could deny the downward-spiralling gravity of the situation. For most people, the preceding decade had had a very real sobering effect. No one had anticipated the failure of reaching agreement on constitutional issues at Meech Lake, or the implications of the new constitution which were being reflected in some Supreme Court decisions. I guess some of us had just naively assumed that things would continue as they were before. And I see now that back in 1981, native issues were not in the forefront the way they should have been; after all, our aboriginal peoples were the first nations on this land mass called North America.

This much more serious attitude was especially noticeable in my meetings with politicians. In 1981 during *Salute to Canada*, many of the political leaders had agreed to appear on our live satellite broadcasts because it seemed like a politically-astute thing to do, but I got the impression that we were viewed as a bit of a nuisance. There had been a kind of cocky confidence that, "We've got the answers, we know what we're doing, we'll fix this country's problems."

Ten years later, I didn't get this feeling at all. There was a new humility. They all knew that our political system was in trouble and they were all eager for prayer.

The Oka and Kanesatake confrontation had put an entirely different complexion on the nation's future. During *Impact Canada 100* there was greater fervency in our prayers, greater realization of the issues at stake for us, and greater understanding that failure to act decisively would topple us to a third-world-nation status.

CHAPTER FIVE

What is the Greatest Crisis Facing the Church Today?

One of the most important features of the *Impact Canada 100* tour was the contact which we initiated with approximately 3,000 church ministers, spouses and full-time Christian workers throughout the nation. Along with undertaking an energetic interdenominational evangelistic thrust across the country, I wanted to stimulate and encourage our Canadian Christian leadership. Each day while we were "on the road", we hosted a luncheon meeting for the local clergy. The fare ranged from roast beef to delicatessen sandwiches to Chinese stir-fries, but the fellowship was uniformly warm and heartening.

Although I've now been involved with television broadcasting for three decades, I still identify with the Christian ministry as a pastor. I think that once a person has a pastor's heart, it's always there as long as one walks closely with God. As an evangelist and as a broadcaster, my goal has never deviated from winning souls for Christ, and immediately doing all I can to get these new believers into a church home, growing and maturing through the spiritual food provided by a God-ordained pastor.

I was especially keen to organize the ministerial meetings for a two-fold purpose: I needed input from the local pastors, and I hoped that I could be an encouragement to them. We wanted to impart to them a sense of shared commitment and challenge, and of belonging to a larger whole across the expanse of Canada.

We obtained input in two ways. Firstly, we gathered information through distributing a questionnaire entitled "Listening to the Heartbeat of Canada's Church Leadership". This survey was designed by Vision 2000 Canada to find out significant patterns in attitudes towards evangelism. The results and insights gained from the nearly 1,000 surveys which we collected are important; they are described later in this book in the Appendix.

Secondly, before lunch was served at the local gatherings, I would tell the clergy members present that we would be discussing four questions around our tables as we ate: (1) What is the greatest crisis facing the church today? (2) What discourages you as a pastor? (3) What encourages you as a pastor? and (4) What is your vision for Canada in the 1990s? Each table would then appoint a chairman to act as spokesman when reporting on the consensus of the group discussions.

As soon as the meal had concluded, I showed a specially-produced videotape which Crossroads had filmed in conjunction with Vision 2000 Canada; it contained thought-provoking observations and comments from a number of well-known Canadian Christian leaders. I then opened the sessions up to a discussion focused on addressing the challenges facing Canada's Christian community in the 1990s.

I was struck by the similarity of responses on so many issues as we moved across the country. On the related topics of "What discourages you as a pastor?" and "What is the greatest crisis facing the church today?," the same words kept recurring over and over: **apathy, complacency, lack of commitment, lukewarmness, loss of vision.**

Roman Catholic Bishop MacDonald reminded us of the scriptural injunction, "Seek ye first the Kingdom of God," and shared with the ministerial gathering at Grand Falls, Nfld., his belief that, "The growing indifference of our people tears the heart out of a minister. We have such a treasure, and yet we don't do much."

Doug Dawson, pastor of Faith Missionary Church in Sault Ste. Marie, Ont., pointed out that some Canadian Christians seem to rank hockey higher than soul winning! He talked about the critical need for believers to prioritize their time commitments.

His thoughts were echoed by Reg Lush, pastor of Cornerstone Christian Centre in Orangeville, Ont., who put it like this, "A lot of church members fill the pews, but leave their Christianity behind at the door. No one outside would even guess that they're Christians." He added, "We're faced with a real lack of spirituality and a need for holiness. People's lifestyles are so busy today that they have too little time for prayer and witnessing."

The Reverend Andre Bourque, a Mennonite Brethren pastor from Quebec, made a similar observation on videotape: "We live in a very materialistic world. Many men and women have to work very hard to pay the bills at the end of the month; those with young families especially lack time for relaxation, for church work and for sharing their faith with their neighbours." He added, "But in the years to come, if we pastors don't teach more equilibrium to church members – how to balance money and faith – we'll miss the boat, because our members won't be able to win their neighbourhood, or their town, or the whole country for Jesus Christ."

I heard ministers from many denominations in many locations say they were often discouraged by the shallowness of belief they encountered, the lack of vision for the lost, the shortage of committed volunteers, and the prevailing "spectator mentality" in which it seemed Christians wanted to be entertained with spiritual fast-food in an "instant McDonalds society".

"Too many church members feel like they've done their bit if they've served on a church committee," said the Reverend Lucas van Boeschoten from Medicine Hat, Alberta. Pastor Harley Johnson of Good Shepherd Lutheran Church in Saskatoon, Sask., pointed out that the root of complacency is the human heart. The pastor at St. Michael's Parish Roman Catholic Church in Swift Current, Saskatchewan, said this about the apathy of Christians: "There's a large gap between what we're called to do and what we're really doing." And Anglican minister, Charles Green from Newfoundland, told us that pastors find it easier to deal with hostility to faith than with apathy.

A number of clergy members, like David Parker of Wellington Pentecostal Church near Belleville, Ont., and Mike Rosenau from the Terrace Christian Fellowship in Terrace, BC, told us that they believed spiritual revival in the pastor's personal life was the key to revival in the church and in the community.

As I listened to these pastors addressing the groups gathered around the tables, I couldn't help harkening back to something from my childhood – the simple truth that enthusiasm breeds enthusiasm. "Do it with all your might," is another time-honoured maxim. And I could never forget what an old preacher told me once, "If there's fire in the pulpit, there will be steam in the pews!"

So, when we all pray, "Revive thy church, oh Lord," perhaps it's the clergy who need to be revived first of all. Let me quickly stress that I'm not saying this to be critical; it applies to me as much as to anyone. But if the clergy had a greater level of fervency in their own lives, their prayer lives, their witnessing for Christ, their pulpit preaching, their involvement in the community... think of the impact that would have on their congregations.

The three levels of belief described in Revelations 3:15 and 16 are equally applicable to people in the pews and to ministers on the platform: "I know your deeds, that you are neither cold nor hot; I would that you were cold or hot. So because you are lukewarm, and neither hot nor cold, I will spit you out of My mouth." If I'm hot for God, it's like the old saying, "Aim for the stars, and you'll at least hit the top of the telephone poles; aim for the top of the telephone poles, and you won't even get off the ground."

To me, that's the way to conquer apathy: to be willing, if necessary, to be thought a fool. I've certainly been considered that many times, and it might be true. But as ministers and as lay Christians, we have to be daring and take initiative.

During *Impact Canada 100,* one of the things I preached in all 100 cities was the message of the cross. Virtually every night the messages were quite different, and I'd often start from a completely different point. But nearly always, I'd end with the scripture portion found in Matthew 16:24 where Jesus says, "If any man come after me, let him deny himself, take up his cross daily and follow me." You know, Solomon said that there was nothing new under the sun. Whatever the present-day problems facing us, we can explore Scriptural principles, and rediscover answers already given to us by God.

In the video shown to pastors, Commissioner Wesley Harris, Territorial Commander of the Salvation Army, encapsulated the situation well: "There are many critical issues facing the church at this time: social issues, the environment, alcoholism, unemployment, poverty, the working poor... But I believe that the greatest issue the church has to face is the spiritual issue, the need of people to find Christ as their personal Saviour. The heart of the human problem is the human heart, and sometimes the church has forgotten that fact. The church's mandate is to proclaim Jesus Christ, and the highest form of community service is to lead a person to Jesus Christ."

In order to call people to commitment and to vision, we have to preach the concept of the centrality of the cross. When people absorb the message of the cross into their spirits, it turns people **to** God and **away** from the secular world. It brings the best out in people. People will give their lives to Christ, give their best to Christ, once the message of the cross really comes into focus for them.

The concept of the cross also includes the fact that the centre of our lives must be outside ourselves. Otherwise, the only thing that's left is self-centredness and selfishness. I think that this is the root of the problem with our national psyche today. Everyone across the country is asking only, "What's in it for me?" And when selfishness is in control, it can only lead to fragmented and competing tribalism, not to any collective efforts at unity.

Earlier this year, the United Nations' annual Human Development Report ranked Canada as the best country in the world for its residents, based upon national income, life expectancy and educational attainment. And in contrast to the United States, the gap between rich and poor did not widen here throughout the 1980s, the so-called "decade of greed". So, we may well have the best country, the best social care system in the world, but people still are not satisfied.

As I look at the situation, it seems that innate selfishness is the overwhelming reason for all the apathy and complaints and negativity we're hearing on a national scale. Let's face it: the great majority of us who tend to "belly-ache" don't actually have an aching belly in this country. Certainly, there are some legitimate concerns. But we're talking about a small fraction of the population who have legitimate griefs about what has, or has not, been done.

For committed Christians, for those with a centredness outside themselves which is anchored in God, their motivating life principle is always translated into unselfish service to others. That's the most effective antidote to apathy and complacency! Just think how things would begin to change on a national scale if more Christians would open their homes and their hearts to **even one** person who has fallen on hard times!

CHAPTER SIX

How Can We Find Solutions for Other Issues?

While lack of commitment, motivation and vision were major problem areas brought up by clergy, a number of other current issues were discussed at our round-table discussions as we criss-crossed the nation during *Impact Canada 100*.

Our surrounding society's attitude that **the church today is irrelevant** was a topic of great concern to everyone present.

During the videotaped messages, the Executive Director of the Evangelical Fellowship of Canada, Brian Stiller, told the pastors his belief that, "The most difficult challenge that faces the church in the '90s is to ensure that the message of Jesus Christ touches people. As a church, we face the obstacle of continuing to live with an ecclesiology or approach out of the past, and we become trapped, either by our denominational or organizational systems. We somehow believe that because it worked in the '50s and '60s, it should work today."

This view was backed-up by the comments of grass-roots pastors. Phil Routley from the Westminster Park Salvation Army Temple in London, Ont., put it simply: "We're not scratching where they're itching!" Pastor Ken Gehrels of the Christian Reformed Church in Collingwood, Ont., talked about the "myopic" and "introspective" nature of so much of the church in Canada.

The Archbishop and Primate of the Anglican Church of Canada, Michael Geoffrey Peers, stated that, "Canadians are more pessimistic than anytime since opinion polling began. And they are even more pessimistic than people in other parts of the Western world. In that sense of a profound lack of confidence, the church is often perceived as just another failing institution. I believe that this represents a major challenge in our time ahead."

The Archbishop's statement was reiterated by many other ministers across Canada. The Reverend Lucas van Boeschoten, a teacher at Hillcrest Christian College in Medicine Hat, remarked that the problem of society's perception is compounded by the church's view of two isolated worlds – Christian and non-Christian. "We've been fear-centred rather than faith-centred for too long," he said.

"The church has been in a maintenance mode for too long," stated Richard Pepper, a Church of Christ minister in Thunder Bay, Ont. Echoed Murray Logan from Grace Mennonite Church in Swift Current, Sask., "The church is like a huge tanker ship that takes a long time and a lot of distance to turn around."

"Do we know our town?," asked Ken Riegert from the Dresden (Ont.) Community Church. This pastor pointed out that our role model, Jesus Christ, met people at their point of need.

"I believe that every church exists for the people who don't belong to it as well as those who do," commented Salvation Army Commissioner Wesley Harris. "I get discouraged when I visit a congregation and sense it is self-sufficient, inward-looking, a kind of sub-culture which is not overly preoccupied with the people, out there, who may think differently. We've got to remind ourselves constantly that we are a people with a mission."

The Reverend George Cunningham told the ministerial gathering in Orillia, Ont., that the church has failed to understand just how irrelevant the rest of society sees it. Another Presbyterian minister, Ron Schroeder from Knox Presbyterian Church in Lloydminster, Alta., said that the church is adapting to culture, and accepting society's values rather than aggressively providing moral standards for the world.

Jeff Kristopher, pastor of First Baptist Church in North Battleford, Sask., observed that because "the church is under a bushel," it's perceived to have no power and therefore – as the TV comedian would say – "God gets no respect."

I believe that one of the best ways to overcome that public image is to make sure that the church in every local neighbourhood is much more than a building located on a certain geographic corner. The church has to be found in the centre of Main Street, involved in all of community life. The pastor and the people have to be "right in there" with everything they have to give.

Don Moore, the Executive Director of Vision 2000 Canada, put it well when he talked about "the unresponsiveness of God's people to impact the community beyond the walls of the church – but those who do, find that they earn the hearing of society." I am one of the many Christians who grew up with a fortress mentality about the church. For years, I thought that the scripture verse, "I will build my church, and the gates of hell will not prevail against it" (Matthew 16:18) meant that we should be huddling inside our church with the gates shut tight so hell could not overcome us.

Even though I had studied this text in the original language in Bible College, like so many other verses, it wasn't until 20 or 30 years later that the truth hit me. Around the time of *Salute to Canada,* I suddenly realized what "gates" really meant. In an agrarian society, where the people went out of the walled city in the morning to work on their farms and returned again each night, the gates were the place of authority where the elders gathered to speak with the people. Since there were no Capital Buildings, the gates were the special places recognized for the political and religious leaders of the day.

This means that the church is not on the defensive; gates never attacked anybody! Instead, we are to be on the offensive, marching on the darkness. Today, God is blasting us out of this fortress mentality with a bold aggressive movement of the Holy Spirit. An East German friend told me about the March For Jesus which recently took place in Berlin; 70,000 to 80,000 Christians with banners and music, dancing and singing "Jesus is Lord" paraded through the Brandenburg Gate, through what used to be the Berlin Wall. That's getting out of the fortress mentality.

To counter society's perception, there also has to be a totally open situation, in which the church is absolutely transparent in terms of its finances, its organization, the personal integrity of its leadership and everything else. As Bill Graham, People's Warden of St. John's Anglican Church in Burns Lake, BC, put it at our meeting, "Integrity in leadership and willingness to compassionately speak out produce loyalty and respect."

Listen to what the Reverend Victor Stonehouse, a Free Methodist Church in Canada minister, said "The thing that concerns me most is the issue of the integrity of leadership. One of the problems we have is that before we can even talk about Jesus, we have to first clean the mud off his face. The church has been given a black eye and Christ has been given a black eye, as leader after leader has fallen. We're now in a kind of recovery mode where we have to demonstrate that Christ living in a leader's life can make a difference, and he or she can be a person of real integrity."

This has been more important than ever since the well-publicized scandals hit the church on both sides of the border during the last decade. But the sad thing is, there have always been scandals in the church since Day One. Just read the epistles of Paul, and you'll soon see that there were things happening there that were worse than all of today's sordid stories put together!

There's no question that a lack of credibility about institutional religion has developed in the public's perception. But this doesn't apply only to religious leaders. From news reports and from everyday conversations, we can sense that Canadians are disenchanted and disdainful of political leaders too, and have lost their faith in politicians' ability to solve the nation's problems.

At this critical time in our country's history when Canadians are questioning basic institutions – including

Confederation itself – I am praying that the church will lead the way in earning respect and credibility. In my experience, I've always found that the best way to overcome incredulousness is to get to know people. If people know you, they'll know they can believe you and trust in you. This is just as true for a national TV ministry as it is for local churches in communities across Canada.

The most important thing to remember is that people are not disillusioned with Jesus Christ and they're not disillusioned with the Scriptures. It's up to each one of us to show by our daily lives and by our actions that the true church is not an organization, not an institution, but a living organism made up of all believers.

* * *

The issues of **family breakdown and moral decline** recurred time after time as the clergy across Canada discussed another crisis facing us today.

The Reverend Elroy Pankratz, a pastor from Antioch Bible Fellowship in Oliver, BC, observed that his congregation has about equal numbers of native and non-native members, but the same family problems are found in everyone's homes.

The pastor at Leamington (Ont.) Pentecostal Church, Victor Grieco, stressed that we can no longer assume people understand the basics of Christianity, because we are faced with "second-generation pagans." He has discovered while conducting funerals that many people can no longer repeat the Lord's Prayer from memory. In an age of pluralism in which everything is tolerated except intolerance, the Reverend Grieco asked us to consider the question of where Christianity fitted in.

Dr. Melvin Sylvester, President of the Christian and Missionary Alliance denomination, told pastors that, "I think the authority of the Scriptures is the critical issue we face. When our world today speaks of truth and falsehood, it is no longer in the traditional or Biblical sense. What was truth yesterday is not necessarily truth today – or what is true for you is not necessarily true for me. Truth for contemporary men and women has become relative."

The Reverend Stuart Silvester, National Extension Secretary of the Fellowship of Evangelical Baptist Churches, added this comment: "The demographic change in our country has evidenced a tremendous shift. Jesus said to go to all the nations, but all the nations have come to us. And we must realize that the majority of people whom we want to reach for Christ are Biblically illiterate and have no foundation of Scriptural knowledge."

We can gain a lot of insight into this current reality by reading the Old Testament books of Judges, I and II Samuel, I and II Kings, I and II Chronicles. These historical accounts make it clear that every three to four generations, if people do not have a living, vital relationship with the God of their fathers, family breakdown and moral decline are inevitable.

"There arose a generation that knew not God": that has happened over and over again. In Scripture and in history texts, every time there has been a breakdown in moral standards, the strength and vitality have been sapped from the culture, and the people have become push-overs for some warring neighbour to come in and make them slaves.

You see, people can get along for a little while on their grandparents' religion. Their parents have taught them Grandma's and Grandpa's moral standards, because even if they didn't have a living relationship with God themselves, they believed that there were absolute standards of right and wrong.

But when you get to the third or fourth generation away from the ancestors who experienced a genuine encounter with the living God which transformed their lives, moral standards crumble and disintegrate. As the minister of Kitimat Presbyterian Church in BC said at the ministerial meeting in his town, people today view the church as a club or a commodity which they only make use of when they need to be "hatched, matched and dispatched." Everyone justifies his or her actions with, "I'm a decent person; I'll do what I want," and the only underlying rationale becomes, "What's in it for me."

Geoffrey Still, President of Focus on the Family (Canada), observed that, "Years ago, you talked in hushed terms about anyone who was divorcing his or her spouse. When I was a teenager, I only knew two people who had been divorced. No one, including non-Christians, supported divorce. But now, people go into marriage with the idea that if it doesn't work out, they will get out of it."

It seems clear that the same social attitudes are affecting prevailing patterns of marriage breakdown. But from a Scriptural basis, if the husband and wife have a centre outside themselves which is found in the Lord, they will acknowledge that the Lord is in their spouse. They will therefore want to do the things which please each other. There are no divorces when that happens, as long as the two walk in harmony. As John Goulding from the Grand Falls (Nfld.) Salvation Army Citadel pointed out, "When we start with a strong family base, we are able to go to our neighbour and to evangelize our community."

Jesus Christ, our Lord, as well as Plato and others, always stressed that belief determines conduct; what you believe is the producer of your standards. So, if you really believe that God thundered the ten commandments from Mount Sinai, that His all-seeing eye is watching your behaviour, that there is going to be judgement... then you're going to think twice about committing anything prohibited by that list. You're going to believe that they really are commandments, and not just "suggestions to be done if it feels good."

You know, I was shocked when I was told that recent statistics indicate that 32 percent of homicides in the United States are committed by juveniles. We have raised a generation with no moral standards. Today, neither the schools, the government nor the media teach morals. Only the church is left to teach moral standards in the community, and we have failed. We can never forget that the church is only one generation away from extinction. If boys and girls don't come to know the Lord, the church is gone, finished, off the scene. But many churches have only half the number of children in Sunday School which they had 10 or 15 years ago. God forgive us; we're failing a whole generation out there, and it's time for us to be aggressive!

So, for many people today, both adults and young people, that core of solid belief is gone. With the eastern and New Age influences, people insist, "I can do anything I please if it makes me feel good and happy." But only when people get their beliefs in order can their lifestyles change. And it's only the Spirit of God who can produce these changes within us.

As Alberta author, scholar and lecturer Maxine Hancock stated, "Committed living runs counter-culture to our current hedonistic age. Our instant-gratification era says that whatever gives me maximum pleasure at this moment is the thing I choose." Instead, she pointed out that, "Committed living, it seems to me, calls us to say, 'No, we look at life as a whole, not as a piece-meal, hour-to-hour thing. We see life as a prelude to eternity. We see life as a sort of vestibule through which we're going to make entry into a much larger space for living. And so we make some choices now that give shape to the whole of life.'"

* * *

One more obstacle pointed out by pastors at virtually every meeting across Canada was the problem of **disunity within the church.**

Brian Stiller outlined the situation: "In our culture, in a world of pluralism, for the government or the media to recognize a particular group of people called evangelical Christians – they can't understand us, because we have 45 denominations. Consequently, we are so badly divided that we have no way of making an impact. But there's another problem," he added, "in that we've become so preoccupied with our own denomination, our own church, our own mission, that sectarianism begins to rule and we become competitive."

The Executive Director of the Evangelical Fellowship of Canada urged listeners to find the balance between wanting to work the best we can, but being unified as expressed by the prayer of Jesus in John 17:21 when He said, 'Father, I will that all of them may be one.'

I have found that denominational barriers drop and cooperation increases whenever we can all gather around the call to evangelism. The bedrock principle is that people need to turn from sin and decide for Christ and make the Lord Jesus their personal Saviour. In my experience, we can always get along with people from whatever Christian denomination on that basis.

The Reverend Victor Stonehouse, a Free Methodist Church in Canada pastor, told Canadian clergy that, "As a pastor, one of the things that really discourages me is the pettiness and smallness which can creep into congregations. I've observed that this happens when a congregation loses its sense of mission. But if something is really captivating their attention, if they're intent on reaching people for Christ, then much of the pettiness just goes by the boards."

Sadly, sometimes there are worse splits internally within congregations than there are between denominations. When people sit in the same pews in the same church but there is disunity, obviously there is an underlying heart problem. Their hearts have to be changed by Christ, and their faith has to be fresh every morning.

Faith can't be something that's 30 years old. That's one of the reasons the Lord laid on my heart for beginning the *100 Huntley Street* ministry. For people who only go to church once or twice a week, we're there with a message from the Lord and a spiritual refreshing every day. I've been told by missionaries working in northern native communities and by many

A ten minute meeting in Prime Minister Brian Mulroney's office turned into a heartfelt exchange, an hour in length, just prior to the beginning of the *Impact Canada 100* tour.

"Tell them to be doers of the Word and not hearers only. Speak up when you see social injustice," NDP leader Audrey McLaughlin.

"We need to think of others; to be more generous and not so selfish," Liberal Party leader, Jean Chretien.

The Impact Canada bus carried the team across the country. Here it's pulling out of the nation's capital ... on to the next city!

"...it certainly was my pleasure to take part in the *Impact Canada 100* tour.... It was an extremely uplifting experience and made me feel good inside," Premier Don Getty, Alberta.

▲ David shares a challenge with the audience at an Impact Canada event inviting them to pray for Canada.

▲ A circle of pastors pray for revival in Canada.

▼ The crowd fills the air with singing.

▲ A life-sized "Vibes," minstrel on the *Kingdom Adventure* television program, greets children.

David in two provinces at once – in Lethbridge, Saskatchewan and Alberta.

Dinner! Courtesy of the Restigouche Indian Reserve, Campbellton, NB, and displayed by Harold Hodgins, the Impact Canada bus driver.

David enjoys a helicopter ride over the Rocky Mountains.

The beauty of the north surrounds the Impact Canada team along the Alaska highway.

The next generation of Canadians proudly wave their national flag.

other people across Canada that this extra daily input is crucial for people struggling to overcome alcoholism, other addictive behaviours and a myriad of personal and family problems.

Of course, Christians who are disciplined in their devotional life, in reading the Word of God and in prayer, don't need *100 Huntley Street* for that reason. As a matter of fact, they should be out visiting shut-ins or doing other ministry work rather than sitting at home watching TV. I only hope that those believers who are mature enough in Christ that they don't need us, also take the time to remember Crossroads with an offering once in a while!

CHAPTER SEVEN

Reasons for Hope and Encouragement as We Face the Future

I don't want you to get the impression that all we discussed at the clergy meetings across Canada were problems. Not at all! We wanted to obtain honest input in order to draw a realistic picture of the current Canadian scene, because only then can we effectively counteract the barriers we face. But the mood was extremely hopeful as we heard countless positive statements of encouragement.

As a matter of fact, many, many pastors pointed out that the mere fact that clergy from a variety of denominations had gathered together to participate in these *Impact Canada 100* clergy meetings and public rallies was a cause for rejoicing. We were able to address common questions, and discover we all had similar problems but shared reasons for hope and inspiration.

Even though ministers had voiced their discouragement about the apathy and lack of commitment found in too many Christians, they also strongly stated that one of their greatest hopes for spiritual revival in the 1990s was found in **lay believers.**

Actually, this seeming dichotomy shouldn't be surprising. That's because both the positive and negative answers to all four questions posed to the ministers (the reasons for discouragement and encouragement, plus the greatest crisis and greatest hope for the '90s) rested on one factor – **people.** While the cold-to-lukewarm spiritual status of some Christians can cause pessimism, the strengths and potential of "hot" Christians are

74

an endless source of hope. And as Pentecostal Assemblies of Canada Pastor Cliff Siebert pointed out during our ministerial meeting in Terrace, BC, God still works in spite of us!

Commissioner Wesley Harris from the Salvation Army put it this way: "Much as I believe that preaching is important, I don't really think that we are going to reach the common man merely with sermonizing from behind the pulpit. The only way we're going to reach the people of our nation with the Gospel – and oh, how they need it – is by mobilizing the laity."

As he observed, "It's so simple and yet it can be so hard to invite your neighbour to church, or to speak to him or her about the joy of the Lord that you experience. But unless we can get our laypeople to do just that, frankly I don't think we have a hope."

A well-known lay leader in the Church of the Nazarene, Marjorie Osborne, who is coordinator of the church-planting thrust 'Target Toronto', told the pastors, "That's one of the most exciting things: I can tell people from personal experience that God is calling laypeople to ministry. And it is an exhilarating way to live in His service, knowing that you are a co-labourer with Him in a specific task."

"One of the things I would cite which is very encouraging to me is the quality of spirit and the measure of commitment that I find on the part of young men and women in our churches across Canada," said Dr. Melvin Sylvester of the Christian and Missionary Alliance. "I see young people today who are courageous, risk-taking types who would surpass, I think, where my peers and I were at when I look back 20 or 25 years ago."

The hundreds of pastors who met with us during *Impact Canada 100* gave hundreds of examples of the growing desire of everyday Christians to get involved in outreach. They cited a groundswell of excitement among young people, a growing network of friends reaching friends, and the emergence of a servant community as the Scriptures came alive to church members with a renewed sense of urgency. As the "laity are turned loose," children are trusting Jesus, families are being restored and recent believers are "hanging in there" with their new-found faith.

The Reverend Alan Braun of Faith Baptist Church in Penticton, B.C., said that he was encouraged to see that, "the church was growing around the kitchen table."

"The Christian community is becoming activated rather than ingrown, and the church is changing without compromise," observed Brian Cowerston, pastor of Faith Missionary Church in Saskatoon, Sask. At the same meeting, the pastor of St. Michael's Parish in Swift Current, stated that he was encouraged by "the resilience of people who come through when the crunch is on, people who live the gospel and think for God." He added, "Limp Christianity is over!"

Mike Rosenau from the Terrace Christian Fellowship in Terrace, BC, told his fellow ministers that the excitement of seeing new believers and of seeing others fitting into God's plans has "people climbing over each other to get involved." He stressed that the size of the task nationally may give us the tendency to wring our hands and ask 'What can we do' – but that starting at the local level can be part of the trigger for the whole country.

I have to confess that when I started in the ministry in the late 1950s, the existing model was for the pastor to do about everything. There has been a very healthy evolution in that regard, because one of the greatest hindrances that ever entered the church was the artificial separation between clergy and laity. Whether you work at an auto assembly plant, or whether funding from a congregation makes it possible for you to give 100% of your time outside the home to Christian ministry, there really isn't any difference in serving the Lord.

Of course, we need to respect leadership within the church, and acknowledge that not everyone is a teacher or an evangelist, but there is definitely something that everybody can do. One of the most effective witnesses I ever knew was a layman named Carl in one of the first churches I pastored. The man had a serious impediment in his speech, and you would have to know him for several months before you could understand what he was saying. Yet, I could look down from behind the pulpit at any given church service, and spot at least 15 people whom he had led to Christ. He brought people to church whom I could never have gotten out to services. What a gift he had!

Today, pastors can take advantage of excellent educational materials for lay believers which were never available in the past. Many national denominations and local bodies across Canada are very involved now in training programs for their lay members. I think the potential is fantastic.

Like my friend, the Reverend Tom Johnstone, said at the recent dedication of the Chapel at the new Crossroads Centre, "I believe not only in the priesthood of preachers, but in the priesthood of all believers." On Judgement Day, we'll all be held responsible for obeying the Great Commission. Ironically, sometimes preachers and evangelists get so caught up in programs and administration and sermon preparation, that they don't have time for personal soul winning.

I'm often amazed at what can be done by dedicated "everyday" believers. We have a janitor of Greek origin named Nick at Crossroads Centre who just led five construction workers to Christ in one week while the building was being completed. If I had tried to preach to those construction guys, the walls would have gone up, but Nick with his mop in one hand and his Bible in the other was able to reach them.

We've got to turn these lay people loose, and then we've got to honour them as heroes of the faith. They're the ones in the trenches every day winning people to Christ.

* * *

Another one of the most encouraging reasons for hope is the increasing **unity** among Christians in Canada. Pastors like Dennis McBride of Delmer Road Baptist in Edmonton and

David Micklist of the Full Gospel Church in Brandon, Man., pointed to *Impact Canada 100* and to the Vision 2000 Canada movement as evidence of peoples' vigorous interest in networking. As its Executive Director, Dr. Don Moore put it, individual Christians, churches and denominations are now working on a common goal, with "unity of purpose but diversity in expression."

The Reverend Stuart Silvester said, "I think as we head into the '90s to do the work of evangelism, the cooperative effort of Vision 2000 Canada is very strategic and very timely. Across our country, among our 500 Fellowship of Evangelical Baptist Churches, there has been a real positive, almost unanimous response saying 'Hey, this type of cooperative work is long overdue.'"

Many of the ministers who met with us told of denominational barriers dropping, of love being evidenced in peoples' lives and of duplicated efforts being transformed into cooperative ventures.

William Cramp from Valley View Free Methodist Church in Sudbury, Ont., said that he sensed increasing church unity and a spirit of cooperation in his community. Pastor Graham Bretherick of the North Side Christian Fellowship in Lethbridge, Alta., stated that he was encouraged to see a commitment to a new unity, with the beginnings of Christians becoming the army of God again.

Hugo Reimer from the Mennonite Brethren Church in Vanderhoof, BC, urged the gathering of clergy to heal hurts. "Don't let the past be a barrier to going on," he said. "Make the church a scent of love." Pastor Lyndon from the Evangelical Free Church in Bonnyville, Alta., expressed hope that in the future we wouldn't be known by our denominational tags, but rather by the fact that we know Jesus.

Tom Mulder, minister of the Sunningdale Associated Gospel Church in Moose Jaw, Sask., remarked that troubled times lead to more openness and to more fresh ideas, as people realize that old structures and methods are not sacred.

Dozens of other pastors gave evidence of a new coalescing of purpose. Richard Pepper, from Church of Christ in Thunder Bay, Ont., told of people wanting to do outreach, of growing unity and youth workers and youth groups who are beginning to meet together in his area. Reg Lush from Cornerstone Christian Centre in Orangeville, Ont., reported that he saw churches and pastors coming together like never before.

Others talked about the increasing fellowship being found among clergy members. Reverend Paul Carr of St. Alban's Anglican Cathedral in Kenora, Ont., pointed to increased communication in his local ministerial association as a sign that God was moving. He expressed his hope that Christians would find strength together in the days before Christ's coming.

Pastor Ron Schroeder of Knox Presbyterian in Lloydminster, Alta., told us that the ministerial association in Lloydminster was "together as never before", working jointly in hospital ministry and other forms of outreach. And Saskatchewan pastor Arnold Lester of the Nepawan Apostolic Church commented that he was encouraged by his local ministerial society. Although it had "taken 10 years to get people together", 16 denominations had cooperated in a recent crusade. "We need more of this," he said, motioning at the pastors sitting around him in Saskatoon.

There's no doubt in my mind. Something is stirring, something new is happening. People across Canada are downplaying denominational differences and maximizing the things we have in common. Those of us who accept the Apostle's Creed and the essential doctrines of the Christian faith have much more in common than any of the relatively small theological differences we may hold.

We need each other. We can learn from each other. The great broad spectrum of people who own Jesus Christ as Saviour are humble believers. We have so much we can teach each other if we take the time to listen.

CHAPTER EIGHT

A Groundswell of Prayer and Revival

Another topic which recurred in our discussions of reasons for encouragement and hope for the '90s was the **growing prayer movement.** Lack of prayer was the number one issue which over three-quarters of the ministers cited as a hindrance to effectively reaching people with the gospel, in the survey which they completed for Vision 2000 Canada during our meetings.

But the situation is turning around. The prayer movement is spreading across our land. People are meeting in small groups and in large, in organized meetings and in spontaneous gatherings, to fervently pray for their families, their churches, their communities, their country. As one pastor put it, "when I stop praying, coincidences stop happening."

Ross Craiger, from the Anglican Church in Huntsville, Ont., told us of a growing emphasis on unity based on prayer and the Bible. Pastor Hugo Reimer from the Mennonite Brethren Church in Vanderhoof, BC, talked about increased initiatives for more prayer.

The Reverend Eric Berg from Steel Heights Baptist in Edmonton, Alta., said, "There's a groundswell of people who are starting to find out what God is saying. There's a hunger and a desperation to find out what God wants, an openness and a willingness to work together. And we're seeing more prayer meetings than ever before."

Pastors told us about more and more churches sensing the need for prayer and for increased emphasis on praise and worship. Thousands are embarking on prayer walks. Concerts of prayer are happening everywhere. In Toronto, the entire SkyDome stadium has recently been filled with an old-fashioned prayer meeting.

The snowballing interest in prayer is one of the major differences I noted in the ten year interval between *Salute to Canada* in 1981 and *Impact Canada 100* in 1991. Of the 100 communities we visited, I found that the pastors of different denominations were already coming together for prayer meetings in over 60 of these centres. Back in 1981, I didn't come across any little cell groups of clergy who were meeting spontaneously for prayer, in groups that had not been officially organized, moved, seconded and voted upon at ministerial associations. Now there seems to be an abandoning of self, an abandoning of a "Party Spirit" amongst the leaders of the churches, and instead a new hunger to come together and pray. To me that was the most encouraging sign of all.

Dr. Don Moore from Vision 2000 Canada stated the case persuasively in the video we showed to pastors: "My vision for Canada is that we would see God's people, once again, called back to their knees in prayer. Because you see, I'm convinced that as you and I, in the quietness and the privacy of our homes, our offices, our kitchens, get on our knees and say, 'God, I don't have clue how to really impact my world – as big or as narrow as that world might be. But God, would you give me an idea? Would you give me a spark that will help me do it? And could I call two or three others around me to pray with me for that idea?'"

He explained, "Because I sense in each community as I've travelled across Canada, as those little sparks ignite, that in fact God is using them in wonderful ways. And as they become living models within communities, others catch that vision. And before long, it filters into the walls of the church. It becomes a church plan for reaching the community. It moves to a regional, denominational level... and before long, we have plans in place for the year 2000 – all because you and I prayed, all because we asked God to inspire us with a fresh vision of what He wants us to do."

* * *

When talking about our hopes for Canada in the 1990's, one more word kept coming up over and over again from the lips of hundreds of pastors: **revival.**

For many of them, this hope was based on their experience of increasing unity, the church's rising sense of responsibility for Canada, and a movement of the Holy Spirit.

Pat Tyler from the Anglican church in Portage La Prairie, Alta., said that he saw the beginnings of the church working together. "Christ is still calling people, and church is becoming more creative after 2000 years," he commented.

Primate Michael Geoffrey Peers from the Anglican Church of Canada told the ministers on our video, "The proclamation of the activity of God revealed in the person of Jesus Christ is crucial... We have to be about the business of demonstrating the presence and power of God."

"The fields are white with harvest and the need is great," Norm Green from North Bramalea United, Ont., reminded us. He also described how the power of God was changing lives, leading to both personal and social transformation.

Some clergy pointed to TV ministries, stating that they were helping Christians and reaching the unseen church. Others, like Jerry Spoor, minister of Vermillion Baptist Church in Alberta, were encouraged by the openness of political leaders to prayer and the moving of God's Spirit in Christian leaders.

Colin Patterson, pastor of the Congregational Church in London, Ont., told us of radical Christianity impacting the community through a powerful moving of the Spirit. Marlene Sarich from the Roman Catholic parish church in Terrace, BC, prayed for a fresh outpouring of the Holy Spirit, because "if we're not on our faces voluntarily, we'll be there involuntarily."

A United Church minister in Bonnyville, Alta., said, "The Holy Spirit is very much alive. I've been 42 years in the pulpit, and I've never seen a hunger for God like I see now."

Eller Gray, from the Anglican Missions to the Lakes District, reassured the Burns Lake, BC, meeting, "We know we are Christ's and He is the Head, and He has promised that He will not fail the church." And George Gruen from the Brethren Missionary Church in Lion's Head, Ont., stated his belief that with so many opportunities around us, Canada will be won!

The Reverend George Grosshans, coordinator of the Decade of Destiny for the Pentecostal Assemblies of Canada, remarked in his videotaped segment, "My greatest encouragement is a sincere hunger for God that we're seeing in so many people. There's almost a desperation in people's search for something they don't have within, which is a spiritual power."

"People do respond, and it has been thrilling to me, both in my own personal witnessing as well as in the corporate ministry, to see God at work in the lives of men and women whom we may have written off," said the Reverend Stuart Silvester of the Fellowship of Evangelical Baptist Churches in the video. "I would say to pastors, "Don't give up. Look to God and realize that He can touch the heart of the hardest person," he added.

I too have found that in many peoples' hearts there's a hunger which the Holy Spirit has produced. My reason for hope is that the hunger and desire is there; that's the beginning for spiritual revival and growth.

I believe according to the Scripture that God responds directly in proportion to the level of our fervency. Let me give you an example. Some people are puzzled about the fact that the three disciples Peter, James and John seemed to be closer to Jesus than all the others. I don't think that Jesus had favorites. I think that He simply responded to the fervency level in these three, which was higher than the other nine.

Scripture tells us that the fervent, effectual prayer of a righteous man or woman avails much, and it also talks about being fervent in spirit as we serve the Lord. Look at it this way:

if God were to respond at a 100% level, but our fervency was only at 50%, then He would be violating our free will. That's the one thing which God will not do; as a matter of fact, I think that to Him, that is the ultimate evil. In contrast, the Devil tries to control us as his slaves, robots and puppets. God wants to set us free to be all He created us to be, and to grow and develop as human beings. He offers us His help if we ask Him, but He never forces us.

So I believe that the level of His blessing, how He gives of His Spirit, is directly proportional to our hunger towards Him and the intensity of our spirits. When I was travelling across Canada for *Impact Canada 100,* I saw a very intense hunger for revival and fervency toward God in the clergy and the laypeople I met, and I was most encouraged by that.

CHAPTER NINE

A Vision for the Next Decade

As I am writing this, the June 8, 1992 issue of *Maclean's* magazine is before me. Its headline trumpets, "Mad as Heck: Why Canadians – Typically – Are Repressing Their Rage."

Let me quote an excerpt from the cover story:

> In a startling reversal, Canadians have lost the sunny optimism that they shared since the end of the Second World War. Few now believe that their lives will become increasingly prosperous or that their children's wealth will surpass their own.
>
> **For many Canadians, that loss of economic faith represents a profound spiritual crisis**. The recession has eroded their fundamental belief in the inevitability of economic progress, but there is no satisfying replacement for that secular faith.
>
> Canadians are resentful, anxious and cynical about their very way of life. In the pollster's language, they are on the cusp of an enormous social change, struggling to accept their reduced prospects, grasping for new certainties and new dreams. Observes Allan Gregg, president of Toronto's Decima Research and *Maclean's* pollster: "It is a seminal sea change from the fairly predictable value system that has been intact for more than 40 years. The idea that 'progress is normal' has been the postwar ethos. Now, there is the realization that past values may no longer be achievable in the future. **But there**

is no replacement ethos. What comes through is borderline despair."

Everywhere today, commentators, journalists, preachers, co-workers and next-door neighbours are saying that they have never seen their fellow Canadians so cynical, so rudderless and full of hopelessness.

It's obvious to me that if this broken country, this broken world, these broken individuals, are going to be fixed, we've got to go directly to the heart of the problem: the human heart. I don't mean that marvellously intricate pump which sustains us from day to day, but our deepest spiritual being.

James, who was known as the brother of Jesus, asked an age-old question: what is the source of the war and fighting and conflict which is emanating from among you? Then he proceeded to detail, in chapter four of his letter, the problems inside each one of us. He describes envy causing quarrelling; wrong motives; pride; arrogance; boasting; and wrongfully judging neighbours. Jesus painted an uncompromising portrait of human nature when he said, "Out of the heart proceed evil thoughts, murders, adulteries, fornications, thefts, blasphemies."

The Bible analyzes the human condition, but even more importantly, it clearly writes the prescription for healing the underlying ailment. When the promises of Scripture are believed and acted on, the ultimate "heart specialist" gives us a new heart (spirit) and transforms us from the inside out.

But He never forces His treatment upon us unwillingly, no matter how life-threatening our condition; He waits for us to ask Him to take on our case. Our God is a lover, not a rapist. He respects us, and even gives us the right to be wrong. He'll never violate the very things which make us human – our intellect, our emotions, our free will – when He offers us his heart-changing, life-giving love. And He won't make us into programmed people, all shaped by the same cookie-cutter. He is a God of infinite variety.

Jesus came to restore each of us individually and to bring us into unity with God. When that relationship with Christ as

Saviour and Lord is alive and real and vital, then selfishness is replaced by caring and getting along with others becomes much more feasible. It gives us a realistic perspective of humanity's frailties and possibilities. The Apostle Paul urged us, "Let each esteem others better than himself." During our meeting, Premier Clyde Wells told me that if we'd all do to others as we would have them do to us, we'd resolve our problems as a nation.

As I was working on this book, I opened the June 10, 1992, edition of *The Globe and Mail*. In it was an account of the convocation address given the day before to graduating students at the University of Toronto by Dr. Murray Frum, husband of the late broadcaster Barbara Frum. Let me share part of it with you:

> What I am certain that Barbara would have wanted to say to you, is that whatever our collective problems, there is something that you can do about them yourself, individually, and that is this: Develop yourself as a thinking and moral being. **Canada will be a better country when Canadians are better people.** And Barbara never doubted the capacity of almost everyone to make him or herself better.
>
> Barbara's idea of what it means to make yourself a better person was both simple and highly demanding. She had little time for grand, sweeping, idealistic talk. Barbara advocated cultivating one's own little patch of ground – one's family, one's friends, one's work – in the belief that civilization is improved by the laying out of one neat garden after another... She also believed that as you work your ground, clearing it, making it beautiful, you may be surprised to discover that you have, after all, changed the world without declaring your intention to do so... Human beings, she believed, were capable of anything.

I was struck by the similarity: a well-known journalist whom I respected very much, Barbara Frum, had been saying the same things I had been proposing throughout *Impact Canada 100* – we could tackle our national problems, making Canada a better country through each of us deciding to become a better person.

Both of these famous Canadians, Clyde Wells and Barbara Frum, were right, of course. But Barbara also talked of "realistically assessing one's fellow human beings." From the lessons of history, from the depths of our own hearts, from the situations around us, we quickly realize the fragility of our best idealistic and altruistic actions – unless they are squarely rooted in a new heart where Jesus Christ dwells. That is the foundational need of every human being. Only Jesus was completely righteous and lived in that totally selfless way; we can live that way only in direct proportion to how much we yield to His Spirit within us.

This is the basic message which I explained to thousands of people as we travelled across Canada one year ago. Did we accomplish what we set out to do with *Impact Canada 100?* My only response can be, "God only knows".

I always visualized *Impact Canada 100* as a kind of catalyst. A catalyst is a chemical agent which is thrown into a potion. It dissolves, it's gone and you can't find it anymore. But it has done what it set out to accomplish. It has sped up the reaction. It has changed the surrounding conditions subtly but unalterably so that something could happen which otherwise would not have been possible.

The whole concept of visiting 100 cities and praying for our country as we travelled across the nation gave me the privilege of meeting personally with our federal and provincial political leaders and praying with them. As far as I'm concerned, that aspect alone was worth the whole effort of undertaking *Impact Canada 100.*

I can say that we had a lot of excitement and enthusiasm most everywhere we went. In some locations, there were fierce snow storms; in Toronto, there was a crippling transit strike; and in places on the prairies, it was 30 to 40 degrees below zero. But I was amazed at the number of people who still made the effort to show up and enthusiastically sing " O Canada". Over 5,000 children and nearly 41,000 adults did just that.

The tour generated a significant amount of media attention and a whole spate of newspaper clippings. We ended up giving close to 200 interviews to radio stations, commercial and cable TV stations and newspapers.

One reporter described the tour as "an upbeat and patriotic presentation to renew faith in a united Canada." Of course, some of the articles were a little sarcastic or incredulous, because I guess some reporters think it's their job to be cynics. But I have a strong feeling that some of the media people who started off cynical didn't end up that way.

You know, I'm not a sophisticated person. I'm just a what-you-see-is-what-you-get kind of Canadian who truly loves his country. I've had the privilege of travelling all over the world through the Crossroads ministry, and I think that Canada is the best country on earth. I wouldn't exchange being a Canadian and living here for citizenship anywhere else – except heaven. Heaven is the only place that's going to be better.

But, strangely enough, I've found that the country which is the best place to live in the whole world is also the place that seems to have some of the most cynical journalists. What I find disturbing is that this type of reporting misrepresents the way people actually are. People may say, "I really don't feel that way, but from what I'm reading I get the impression that all other Canadians feel negatively about this – so I guess I should too."

I just want to tell everyone: all other Canadians do not feel pessimistic. From coast to coast, I've met Canadians who love this land, and I'm convinced that they are the ones in the majority. They knew that we've got the best country in the world, even before the United Nations made it official in 1992, and they want to preserve it.

Most of the media coverage mentioned *Impact Canada 100's* theme of praying for Canada. Canada Press headlines said, "Evangelist Mainse says prayer will help nation find identity" and "We've tried many things, but what about prayer." *The Winnipeg Free Press* reported, "Part of the treatment for what ails the country, Mainse says, can be found in prayer because prayer carries hope. 'When people pray, they become optimistic. There's always hope with it.'"

Those of us who believe the line from Coleridge, "More things are wrought by prayer than this world dreams of," can grasp the crucial importance of praying for our country, night after night. At almost every rally, at least 11 different clergy members would lead the congregation in prayer. In some locations, we had virtually 100% of the clergy gathered together. I don't like using the terms "mainline" or "sideline" to describe denominational affiliations; let's just say we were all Christians who joyfully affirmed the Apostle's Creed. We had the opportunity of meeting nearly 3,000 of these ministers of the Gospel as we travelled across the land.

During the noon-hour luncheon meetings for local pastors, I would pass around the *A Call to Prayer* booklet which we would be using that night. The clergy members were given the choice of either reading from the brief prayers which I had prepared for the booklet, or of using their own words to express the particular thought. Many times we were able to include native clergy in this group of leaders. Some of the pastors rewrote beautiful prayers; I only wish I was able to write as well. But *A Call to Prayer* represented my own feeble effort, because I wanted to ensure that we didn't miss any important subjects each night. The nightly prayer time became one of the highlights of the tour; I found it incredibly moving to pray to our Heavenly Father along with many other believers in Christ.

These prayers have not suddenly become outdated; neither do they have to be used in large auditoriums with hundreds of people taking part. Perhaps you'd like to use them with members of your own family, in your small group Bible study or at church. Or, you can read them softly to yourself during your own personal times of Bible reading and prayer. After all, the power of intercessory prayer continues, long after tours like *Impact Canada 100* have become part of history.

A Commitment to Canada

We, who pray "God Keep Our Land" every time we sing "O Canada", believe that He will keep our land. We believe that our prayers, individually and corporately, will make the difference. We give thanks to God for the freedoms we enjoy, and we determine to love and respect our neighbour, as we would have our neighbour love and respect us. And since it is only God's grace which enables men to change their hearts toward one another, we therefore further determine to share His love and truth with our fellow Canadians.

Responsive Prayer

Leader: We, who are citizens of Canada, humbly ask You, O God, to look upon us with mercy and grace. From your Word in the Seventy-second Psalm, our founding fathers took this motto:

All: "He shall have Dominion also from sea to sea and from the river to the ends of the earth."

Leader: We thank you, O God, that they recognized that You are over us as a people. We thank you that their descendants, aware of our need of Your assistance, asked You to govern in the affairs of men, including in our National Anthem these words:

All: God Keep Our Land.

Leader: Sometimes we are tempted to lose faith in our leaders and institutions. And so we pray, as Paul directed in his first letter to Timothy, for "all who are in authority, that we may lead a quiet and peaceable life in all goodness and reverence."

All: God Keep Our Land.

Leader: We acknowledge, O God, that the family was the first institution You created. That institution is now sorely beset, and we need Your help. Intervene in strained marriages. Turn the hearts of parents to their children, and children to their parents. And save all family members from abuse of any kind, that our homes might be safe places of refuge and Christian love.

All: God Keep Our Land.

Leader: O Lord, make us sensitive to the needs of others, to those who are without work and unable to care for their loved ones. For all who are ill in body, mind, soul and spirit, send your healing power to restore them.

All: God, come in miracle-working power.

Leader: In these uncertain and perilous times, there are so many temptations to be fearful. Recall to our minds, O God, all the nations who turned to You in great need. You preserved and delivered them. Give wisdom and courage and patience to all.

All: God Keep Our Land.

Leader: Lord, you gave our first parents "Dominion over our creation." You entrusted them with the loving care of all nature. Modern man has forgotten that charge. Help us now to reverse the destruction caused by greed and restore our environment.

All: God Keep Our Land.

Leader: We pray for peace among all the nations of this planet. We pray that you would touch the hearts of leaders and turn them to the path of peace. And at home we pray for peace between the peoples of Canada. Give each of us mercy and compassion in our hearts, that we might love our neighbours as ourselves.

All: God, grant us peace.

Leader: O Lord, we pray for the native peoples in our Land. May hurts be healed and full recognition of all the founding peoples be granted.

All: God, bless our native people.

Leader: O God, for those of us who pray these prayers, pour out your Spirit upon us, that we may turn from our own way and go Your way – more faithfully than ever before.

All: God, keep us true to You.

Leader: And finally, O Lord grant that we as Christians may have the courage to proclaim and act upon the Word of God.

All: God, grant us courage.

I am confident that the long-term results of *Impact Canada 100* will be more significant than anything we may perceive from our temporal vantage point. Certainly, the 1,047 people who came forward to register decisions for Christ made the tour eternally worthwhile, if for no other reason.

To me, the concept of a catalyst is the most apt illustration to convey how I feel when reflecting back on *Impact Canada 100*. A catalyst may seem to have disappeared, but it has made all the difference in the world to the final outcome. I think we've been like that. We've gone out into this great spiritual, moral, emotional, political reaction which has been happening all across Canada, and we've put in a word for Christ. And I trust God that there will be a difference because of what we did.

Now as we mark another milestone in the history of our great nation and look toward the decade ahead, it's up to each one of us to decide how we can make a difference within our own spheres of influence. As we interact within our own families, churches, workplaces and communities, each of us can, within our own small circle of relationships, foster a sense of unity through our actions and attitudes.

Tolerance is the by-word for the '90s, but we can do more than just tolerate. We can extend a love and understanding to our neighbour. When we see social injustice, we can speak out and act on it and live out our responsibility to our fellow Canadians. We can take a stand in support of our political leaders. Instead of criticizing the system and the individuals in leadership positions, we can vote for them and uphold them in our conversations. Above all, we can pray for them and ask God to direct their thoughts and decisions according to His will.

Change is possible, and it starts with me and you. Let us all pledge to individually be catalysts for it. Join me now to pray for God's guidance that each of us might act with increasingly Christ-like justice and compassion. Thus we will truly impact Canada and watch unity grow from sea to sea.

APPENDIX

Listening to the Heartbeat of Canada's Church Leadership: What the Survey Told Us

As I stated in earlier chapters of this book, a key aspect of the pastors' meetings which we conducted in 100 communities during *Impact Canada 100* was obtaining input and ideas. In addition to our round-table discussions, we distributed a questionnaire entitled *Listening to the Heartbeat of Canada's Church Leadership*. This survey, designed by Vision 2000 Canada, asked 10 questions aimed at developing a national perspective on what's currently being done to reach our nation for Christ.

First, let me explain a little bit about what Vision 2000 Canada is. It's a movement of over 60 denominations and Christian organizations across our nation, including Crossroads Christian Communications Inc. It seeks to serve the body of Christ so that every person in Canada will have the opportunity to see, hear and respond to the Gospel by the year 2000.

Through its four-pronged mandate, it aims to mobilize Christians across the country by –

Vision: by informing one another of critical needs and opportunities for evangelism

Hope: by inspiring one another with illustrations of what God's people are doing in evangelism

Commitment: by influencing one another to making evangelism a high priority in our ministries

Cooperation: by involving one another in evangelism initiatives and networking which will strengthen our individual evangelism efforts.

As you can see, these goals corresponded with the underlying philosophy of our *Impact Canada 100* thrust. So, we were very pleased to work in tandem with Vision 2000 Canada in distributing the surveys, with the net result that nearly 1,000 questionnaires were completed. This sizable sampling of Canadian clergy is providing church leaders involved in Vision 2000 Canada with invaluable information in formulating evangelism strategies at the local, regional and national level.

Just before we went to press with this book, Vision 2000 Canada obtained the final result tabulations, along with comments on the findings from a dozen Canadian church leaders. Because we believe that the survey results are significant to future plans for impacting our nation for Christ, we are printing the article here, with Vision 2000 Canada's permission.

More than three-quarters (77%) of pastors responding cited lack of prayer as the greatest hindrance to effective evangelism, followed by lack of motivation (68%) and lack of vision (65%). Those figures don't surprise Eric Stolte, on staff with the Navigators in Saskatoon. Stolte has been instrumental in establishing regular prayer meetings among Christian leaders in Saskatoon, and organized a pastor's prayer summit there a few months ago. Since prayer for the city has become a priority, leaders have noticed an increased response in individual ministries. Malcolm Beckett, director of evangelism for the Atlantic United Baptist Convention, agrees with the findings. "We basically play at prayer," he comments. But like in Saskatoon, in Atlantic Canada things are also changing, because "People are seeing the need of prayer."

Stolte sees the lack of prayer, motivation and vision cited by pastors as all part of the same package. "All three are just a lack of hope," he suggests. Coming together in prayer, he says, inspires hope, "which will create motivation and vision."

"The lack of prayer is clearly evident as I travel across the country, says Bill McRae, chancellor of Ontario Bible College/Ontario Theological Seminary and chairman of Vision 2000. But he says he is "very hopeful, very optimistic and very impressed" with the way prayer is being seen as a priority in some places. "There is a really significant resurgence of prayer."

Don Moore, executive director of Vision 2000, has also seen encouraging signs of prayer in action. "My observation has been that currently across Canada, we're experiencing a widespread, informal network of praying beginning to take place."

Beckett say lack of vision characterizes the church in his experience. "We're very much focused on what's going on inside the church. I don't think people even understand what a vision is."

Both McRae and Stolte also add disunity as a factor hindering evangelism. "We bring a gospel of reconciliation, when in fact we are not reconciled ourselves," says Stolte. Adds McRae, "One of the major, major obstacles is that everybody is playing their own game." On the positive side of that coin, Stolte says unity is becoming evident in Saskatoon. "One of the pastors was saying we're not really pastors of individual churches; we're associate pastors of one church. That's miraculous."

Queried on the methods used to evangelize, nearly 86 per cent of pastors responded that regular church services are the primary means of evangelism, followed by personal evangelism (83%), and special events (77%). But often these methods cannot be divorced from each other, comments David Macfarlane, pastor of Islington Evangel Centre in Toronto. "Our experience here with personal evangelism is that it is the bridge that brings people to church," he explains. To him the method is not an "either/or," but a process. At Islington, people come to Christ every week, he adds, whether they are invited by friends or come in off the street. But McRae is uncertain of the value of using church services as the primary means to evangelize. "That probably explains why there are so few coming to the Lord," he says. If church services are being used for evangelism, he points out, they must be "user-friendly," that is, geared especially to those who are not Christians.

"I think we know the traffic of life is not coming in the front door of the church," adds Don Posterski, who heads

World Vision of Canada's domestic ministries. After spending many years with Inter-Varsity Christian Fellowship, Posterski sees relationships as a vital part of any process. "We know what produces the fruit of evangelism: It comes out of relationship and it comes out of serving people's needs in crisis and giving them a safe place to seek the spiritual."

Noting that door-to-door contact was the second-last most popular method of evangelism next to television and radio, Macfarlane nevertheless sees value in that method. Leaving a written invitation at someone's door, he says, is like leaving a "time bomb": some time down the road a person might have a crisis and remember the invitation.

Moore sums up the diversity of methods this way: "There has been an increased awareness as to the importance of a multiplicity of approaches to evangelism. Not everyone will feel comfortable about all approaches." Individuals should be affirmed in their own approaches, he suggests.

Pastors surveyed were also asked about the means that may help stimulate involvement and commitment to evangelism. A majority (76%) listed effective models as an important means, followed by training seminars for church evangelism (75%) and training seminars for community outreach (72%). But even good models can only do part of the job, according to some Christian leaders. Models must deal with the barriers cited earlier, points out Glenn Smith, executive director of Christian Direction in Montreal. Ken Driedger, pastor of Portage Alliance Church in Portage La Prairie, Manitoba, adds that models are important but can only be effective if the motivation is there. And motivation, he notes, comes from the Holy Spirit. Posterski sees models as important, "because people are saying 'we're not seeing very much of it happen, so show me and that will give me some prototypes and patterns."

Training, listed by three-quarters of pastors as an important means to stimulate commitment to evangelism, also elicits skepticism from a few leaders. "I understand why people say that but I'd move that one way, way down on the list," says Smith, noting that numerous training seminars and conferences have been created already. McRae, however, says there should be an emphasis on training. "My fear is that we have not done an adequate job of training people in personal evangelism." Beckett gives a qualified response to the need for training. The problem with training seminars, he points out, is that after they're over, more often than not the information gets lost and people carry on with their lives. He suggests a six-week follow-up, so the content of the training is kept before people, with "almost an accountability." But, he adds, "the motivation has to be there first."

Fewer than half (43%) of the pastors responding said they have a defined strategy for evangelism. Yet strategy is "essential," says Driedger, if a church is to evangelize. Smith indicates some surprise at the low percentage. "I would have thought that in these days of emphasis on strategy and on method and on the machine, it would be higher," he comments. While acknowledging the importance of strategy, his view is that "far too many strategies are created in boardrooms. We don't dare think about the re-evangelization of Canada without thinking about strategy, but strategy must be done on the streets." And where churches do have strategies, McRae reflects, in many cases they "need to be carefully reviewed in terms of their effectiveness."

In the Maritimes, notes Beckett, strategy has changed little over the last century. About 80-85% of Atlantic Canada's 560 Baptist churches were organized before 1900. A revival was sweeping the area, and churches grew out of the crusades: a travelling evangelist would come to town, there would be 50 or so conversions, and a church would form. Until Beckett was appointed, a convention evangelist was expected to carry out the bulk of evangelism. As one who oversees rather than does all the work himself, Beckett is trying to overcome the notion people have that evangelism "is something you do one week or two weeks out of the year."

Churches do need to have a strategy, says Moore, but "strategy has to be built around a vision." His comment reflects what others say about methods and vision. "Somehow we've got to create a more clear statement of why we exist and how we respond."

Asked about compassionate ministries and priorities, 68% of pastors said financial assistance was the most common type of help, followed by food distribution (65%) and clothing distribution (45%). "I wish it wasn't the top one," responds Marjorie Osborne to the emphasis on financial help. "I think contact with the people that need the help is really important." Osborne, coordinator of church growth in Canada for the Church of the Nazarene, has made compassionate ministry a vital part of that work. But she sees compassion not just as handing over money and supplies to the poor. "It's the transmission of the love of Christ from one person to another that really seems to bring hope." Sitting down and chatting with someone makes a huge difference, Toronto-based Osborne says. An example: one man receiving clothing couldn't read the tags to know how many "points" he was spending. "I lent him my reading glasses," says Osborne. She also gave him a ride home. "Later he said he couldn't get over the fact that there is a food bank in the city that would give a person a ride home. His life has turned around."

Osborne suggests compassionate ministry must be based on need. In one community, it might be a daycare; in another, helping refugees; in another, counselling.

Others would agree that compassion is part and parcel of evangelism. "The largest front door for evangelism that we have," says Driedger, "is counselling those who have had a sexually abused past." In his community, the church has made friends with the people who run the women's shelter and family services. "In our need-meeting of caring for those people, we've seen countless families come to Christ."

Like Osborne and Driedger, Posterski, who oversees World Vision's NeighbourLink program that coordinates church volunteers to respond to local needs, sees the importance of contextualizing compassion. "It seems to me that churches need to study the neighborhoods where they are," he says. Moore agrees. "I'm noticing there are a number of significant models of churches looking at how they can influence the quality of life in their communities."

Leaders commenting on the survey findings feel that many factors – prayers, motivation, vision, relationships, compassion – work together. Strategy can only be effective if a vision has been articulated. People generally only respond to Christ because of a relationship with a person, and relationships only work when there is motivation.

Written by Debra Fieguth
Used by permission of Vision 2000 Canada

ABOUT THE AUTHORS

David Mainse is an ordained minister in the Pentecostal Assemblies of Canada. He graduated from Eastern Pentecostal Bible College in Peterborough, Ont., and pastored churches in Brighton, Chalk River, Deep River and Hamilton, Ont. for 18 years.

His early beginnings in television broadcasting in 1962 expanded to weekly half-hour programs known as *Crossroads,* before the daily live *100 Huntley Street* program went on-air in June, 1977. In 1992, Crossroads Christian Communications Inc. celebrated its thirtieth anniversary with the opening of a state-of-the-art broadcast production facility in Burlington, Ont.

As founder and president, David Mainse oversees this diversified, non-denominational, non-profit family of ministries, which now envelopes wide-ranging activities around the globe. These include nation-wide telephone counselling centres, Heart to Heart Counselling Services, Circle Square Ranches for children, emergency relief and development efforts, the *Kingdom Adventure* children's series, foreign language broadcasts for Canadian and overseas audiences, assistance with the development of indigenous Christian broadcasting in Western and Eastern Europe, and the training of Russian nationals and East Europeans in production and counselling techniques through the Broadcast Academy at Crossroads Centre.

He has travelled extensively, including numerous visits to the sites of the highly-acclaimed Pavilion of Promise, featuring "The Scroll" musical, at World Expositions in Vancouver, Brisbane and Seville. He continues to hold evangelistic crusades and is a member of the Fellowship of Canadian Itinerant Evangelists. He has addressed numerous conferences, including National Religious Broadcasters in Washington, D.C., Vision 2000 Canada in Ottawa, and the Liberal Forum of Ontario. He has served on a number of advisory boards, including the international panel of judges for the Templeton Prize for Progress in Religion.

David and his wife of 35 years, Norma-Jean, live in a farmhouse in the rolling countryside near St. George, Ontario, where Norma-Jean was born. They are the parents of four children, and the grandparents of eleven. They attend Evangel Pentecostal Church in Brantford.

Wendy Elaine Nelles is a ninth-generation Canadian whose French Huguenot and United Empire Loyalist roots have enriched her appreciation of her country's heritage. She grew up on her family's century farm near Scotland, Ont. She was awarded department medals for highest academic achievement in English Literature and Psychology upon earning her B.A. from Wilfrid Laurier University, Waterloo, Ont. She also holds a Master of Arts degree in Communications with high honour from Wheaton College, Illinois, where she was conferred the department award for leadership and academic distinction.

She has freelanced for a number of Christian organizations, and was invited to join the broadcast media staff at two international conferences for itinerant evangelists in Amsterdam, sponsored by the Billy Graham Evangelistic Association. Her byline has appeared in a variety of Canadian and American Christian publications, including *The Centurion* magazine published by Crossroads Christian Communications Inc.

Wendy also utilizes her writing, editing and public speaking skills as a specialist in underwriting research and development at the international headquarters of a life insurance corporation. She is an advisory board member of the *God Uses Ink* Christian Writers Conference sponsored by the Evangelical Fellowship of Canada, and has served as a deacon and chairman of outreach programs at Yorkminster Park Baptist Church, a large urban congregation in Toronto.